# Palgrave Studies in Economic History

Series Editor
Kent Deng
London School of Economics
London, UK

Palgrave Studies in Economic History is designed to illuminate and enrich our understanding of economies and economic phenomena of the past. The series covers a vast range of topics including financial history, labour history, development economics, commercialisation, urbanisation, industrialisation, modernisation, globalisation, and changes in world economic orders.

More information about this series at
http://www.palgrave.com/gp/series/14632

Patrick Karl O'Brien

# The Economies of Imperial China and Western Europe

Debating the Great Divergence

Patrick Karl O'Brien
Department of Economic History
London School of Economics
and Political Science
Oxford, UK

ISSN 2662-6497          ISSN 2662-6500 (electronic)
Palgrave Studies in Economic History
ISBN 978-3-030-54613-7          ISBN 978-3-030-54614-4 (eBook)
https://doi.org/10.1007/978-3-030-54614-4

© The Editor(s) (if applicable) and The Author(s), under exclusive license to Springer Nature Switzerland AG 2020, corrected publication 2021
This work is subject to copyright. All rights are solely and exclusively licensed by the Publisher, whether the whole or part of the material is concerned, specifically the rights of translation, reprinting, reuse of illustrations, recitation, broadcasting, reproduction on microfilms or in any other physical way, and transmission or information storage and retrieval, electronic adaptation, computer software, or by similar or dissimilar methodology now known or hereafter developed.
The use of general descriptive names, registered names, trademarks, service marks, etc. in this publication does not imply, even in the absence of a specific statement, that such names are exempt from the relevant protective laws and regulations and therefore free for general use.
The publisher, the authors and the editors are safe to assume that the advice and information in this book are believed to be true and accurate at the date of publication. Neither the publisher nor the authors or the editors give a warranty, expressed or implied, with respect to the material contained herein or for any errors or omissions that may have been made. The publisher remains neutral with regard to jurisdictional claims in published maps and institutional affiliations.

Cover credit: Craig Hallewell/Alamy Stock Photo

This Palgrave Macmillan imprint is published by the registered company Springer Nature Switzerland AG
The registered company address is: Gewerbestrasse 11, 6330 Cham, Switzerland

*In memorium to Cassy and I hope this book will promote further and future conversations with my friends and fellow economic historians: Bob Allen and Peer Vries*

# Preface and Acknowledgments

My late career as an economic historian has remained intellectually exciting and socially enjoyable largely because years ago I decided to reallocate more of my reading and research time into an engagement with global economic history. That occurred at a time of "globalization" when that field was moving from a stage of imminence to prominence in history departments of major universities throughout the world. The revival of this style of history in a comparative form, depends very heavily on intellectual collaboration among colleagues and friends who wish to share the specialized knowledge they have acquired from their studies of the economies, polities and cultures of Afro-Asian and South American cultures.

I was singularly fortunate when I decided to move my research and reading away from British and European economic history to become a Fellow at St Antony's College in the University of Oxford, working among a group of colleagues with the linguistic credentials and distinguished scholarly records derived from their specialized research on the economies of China (Mark Elvin); India (Tapan Raychaudhuri);

---

The original version of the book was revised: Additional corrections have been updated in the chapters. Corrections to the book are available at https://doi.org/10.1007/978-3-030-54614-4_8

viii PREFACE AND ACKNOWLEDGMENTS

Islamdom (Roger Owen); Japan (Ann Waswo); Russia (Angus Walker) and South America (Jeremy Adelman).

My network of influential colleagues widened when I was invited by the late Jerry Martin (Chairman of the Renaissance Trust) to participate in a sequence of conferences and workshops convened to analyse and discuss "Achievements and Creativity" in the interrelated histories of Western science, technological innovation, cities, art and economic progress. At workshops and conferences (convened and coached by Jerry Martin a distinguished engineer, inventor and entrepreneur) academics from several disciplines remote from economic history engaged in heuristic discourses about the history of innovation. They (Margaret Boden, Alan Macfarlane, Steven Shapin, Robert Fox, Simon Schaffer, Rob Iliffe, Ian Inkster, Penny Gouk) and their networks educated me in "ways of knowing and understanding" economic growth from new intellectual perspectives. That phase of education proved to be extremely useful when I obtained grants from the Leverhulme Trust and the European Science Foundation to convene collaborative programmes of research and discourse at the London School of Economics in the, by then, established and expanding field of Global Economic History.

Networking across continents as well as the boundaries of universities and disciplines has kept me in regular, helpful and heuristic contact with leading members of the California School (Roy Bin Wong, Ken Pomeranz, Roberts Marks, Jack Goldstone). And in touch with distinguished groups of historians with expertise on the long-run development of the many regions of our global economy. That peer group included: Peer Vries, Maarten Prak, Jan-Luiten Van Zanden, Matthias Middell, Stephen Broadberry, Maxine Berg, Giorgio Riello, Bartolomé Yun-Casalilla, Eric Vanhaute for Europe. For India, I have been privileged to enjoy connexions with Prasannan Parthasarthi, Tirthankar Roy and David Washbrook. For Africa with Gareth Austin. For China with Kent Deng, Mark Elvin, Bozhong Li, Richard Von Glahn and Harriet Zurndorfer. For Latin America, Alejandra Irigoin and Regina Grafe. For Japan, Penelope Francks, Kaoru Sugihara and Shigeru Akita and for everywhere with Gervaise Clarence-Smith.

Many more names could and should be listed of academics who have shared my aspiration for the revival of metanarratives in global economic history and who have recognized the need for collaborative, cross-disciplinary research, discourse and debate in order to refine, deepen and diffuse that aspiration. I thank them all for the education, ideas and insights that have enabled me to create an impression that I know something about the economic histories of several parts of our globalizing economy and to write this book. All our books are collective endeavours, but I owe a special word of thanks to the California School for creating a famous controversy around the Great Divergence which informs and permeates the chapters of this Palgrave Pivot. Above all I am truly grateful to my friends and mentors, Mark Elvin and Kent Deng. They have patiently and unselfishly shared with an "outsider" and mere amateur their extraordinary range of erudition on all the complex forces and factors (including that important climacteric in science and technology) that maintained the economy of Imperial China on a trajectory for political and institutional development that led to centuries of prolonged divergence with the West.

Finally, I must convey my appreciation to two top administrators (Lorraine Long and Priscilla Frost). They have carried the essential logistical burdens involved in the organization of enterprises in academic collaboration across frontiers of countries and boundaries of universities with discretion, charm and efficiency.

Oxford, UK                                                    Patrick Karl O'Brien
July 2021

# PRAISE FOR *THE ECONOMIES OF IMPERIAL CHINA AND WESTERN EUROPE*

"No scholar has done more to promote global economic history than Patrick O'Brien. In this brief but dense text he presents his position in the biggest debate in that field. He analyses why China, long the world's most advanced organic economy, was overtaken by industrializing Western Europe. His main explanation is endogenous: The country depleted its natural endowment and its government did hardly anything about it. I agree."

—Peer Vries, *International Institute of Social History, Amsterdam*

"Patrick O'Brien has led the renaissance of global history, especially global economic history, in Europe. This energetically written book is a masterly expression of his erudition and argumentative incisiveness as he synthesises and dissects the Great Divergence debate of the last twenty years."

—Gareth Austin, *Professor of Economic History, University of Cambridge*

# CONTENTS

| | | |
|---|---|---|
| 1 | Historiographical Context and Bibliographical Guide | 1 |
| 2 | Statistical Bases for a Chronology of Economic Divergence Between Imperial China and Western Europe, 1638–1839 | 17 |
| 3 | Environments and Natural Resources | 31 |
| 4 | The Ming and Qing Imperial States and Their Agrarian Economies | 47 |
| 5 | SinoCentred Reciprocal Comparisons of Europe's and China's: Economic Growth 1650–1850 | 69 |
| 6 | Cosmographies for the Discovery, Development and Diffusion of Useful and Reliable Knowledge in Europe and China | 91 |
| 7 | Debatable Conclusions | 109 |

**Correction to: The Economies of Imperial China and Western Europe**     C1

**Index**     115

CHAPTER 1

# Historiographical Context and Bibliographical Guide

**Abstract** This chapter reminds readers that the recent rise in the volume of publications in the economic history of Imperial China has been promoted by the extraordinarily rapid rate of economic growth achieved by the Peoples' Republic over the last forty years. The economic and, by implication, the geopolitical advance of communist China to a position of eminence within and significance for the growth of the world economy at large has raised the meta historical question of when, how and why did the Chinese economy decline into a condition of relative backwardness compared with advanced modern economies of Western Europe, North America, Australasia and Japan? The question remains germane and salient because western views of the Chinese state economy and society were (as historiographical surveys reveal) almost entirely favourable before the eras of industrialization and enlightenment in Western Europe. Thereafter western intellectuals entertained increasingly negative perceptions of Chinese civilization that degenerated into Eurocentric levels of denigration and contempt before 1914. Although Eurocentrism became less common in the wake of the barbarous conflicts of the twentieth century, condescension continued until the Chinese economy revealed its underlying potential for modern economic growth after the death of Mao in 1976. Thus, the protracted debate on the Great Divergence can be represented as a controversy inspired by a generation of Sinologists who have attempted with some success to rescue the economic history of Imperial

© The Author(s), under exclusive license to Springer Nature
Switzerland AG 2020
P. K. O'Brien, *The Economies of Imperial China
and Western Europe*, Palgrave Studies in Economic
History, https://doi.org/10.1007/978-3-030-54614-4_1

1

China from a Western tradition of writing that history as one of decline and retardation. The following chapters written by an economic historian of Europe locate this famous debate in historiographical context and are also offered as a survey and critique of that laudable (and for global and comparative economic history) highly provocative, stimulating and heuristic endeavour.

**Keywords** Divergence · Convergence · Growth · Retardation · Stasis · Historiography · Malthusian · Marx · Weber · Elvin · Pomeranz · California school

The "Great Divergence" is the widely known and short title of a seminal book published at the turn of the millennium by America's most distinguished historian of late Imperial China. Almost immediately the book by Ken Pomeranz became the focus for an ongoing controversy for global history, economics and politics (Pomeranz 2000; *American Historical Review Forum* 2002; *Journal of Asian Studies* 2002, 2003; Ringmar 2007; *Canadian Journal of Sociology* 2008; Vries 2015).

First, because it reminds us to review historical antecedents for the People's Republic's recent and extraordinarily rapid convergence towards levels of economic superiority that the West had supposedly established over China some three or four centuries ago (Grinin and Korotayev 2015). The communist regime's success in lifting millions of its citizens out of an age-old condition of poverty has been truly outstanding (Eckstein 1968).

On average, real incomes may have multiplied more than 4–5 times since the death of Mao in 1976. Currently, the economy produces around 20% of the world's output of commodities and services. If present trends continue, the Chinese people could conceivably enjoy American standards of living before the end of this century (Deng 2016).

Secondly, China's recent and remarkable economic advance which has coincided with a greater rate and intensity of participation of virtually all national economies in the process of globalization has also promoted the revival of a long-standing debate among European, American, Japanese, Indian and Chinese intellectuals concerned to explain when, how and why an enormous gap in levels of material welfare opened up between occidental and oriental societies (Perez and De Sousa 2018). That debate is located in a now fashionable interest in world history, which transcends material welfare to include all aspects of political, social, moral, cultural, as well as economic histories concerned with the rise, decline and qualities of civilizations (Frank 1998; Vries 2013). Apart from current preoccupations with Islam, the Asian civilizations that have attracted, prolonged and serious attention are China, Japan and India (Parthasarathi 2010; Eichengreen et al. 2010; Francks 2016; Vries 2020). The modern debate on economic divergence has, however, remained heavily concentrated upon China, basically because, for several centuries before 1700 Europeans retained a view of Chinese civilization that was almost universally favourable (Phillips 1998; Jones 2013). Thereafter, and as adverse contrasts between the productivity of the empire's economy, differences in standards of living afflicting its population and the backwardness of its technologies for production and warfare became discernible, then visible and eventually stark, western commentaries on China became dominated by narratives of retardation. These Eurocentric narratives implicitly or explicitly lauded the rise and superiorities of the west and found explanations for the decline of the east by drawing contrasts between the political systems, institutions, legal frameworks and cultures, promoting (and for the Chinese case) obstructing historical trajectories for long-term economic progress (Dawson 1967; Brook and Blue 1999).

Needless to say, such views remained an anathema to Ming and Qing emperors and their mandarin officials. Until the fall of the empire in 1911 and long after a humiliating defeat by Britain in the Opium War 1839–1842, they continued to reject any suggestion that China's economic institutions and technological knowledge, let alone its political constitution and moral values had anything significant to learn from the west (Wright 1957). For example, and just three decades after the takeover of Bengal by a private multinational corporation—the British East India Company—which was followed by the collapse of the Mughal empire not far away in South Asia—Lord Macartney (who led a failed diplomatic mission to negotiate more flexible terms for commercial relations between the United Kingdom and China) was told in 1800 by the Emperor that "our Celestial Empire possesses all things in prolific abundance and lacks not product within its borders. There is, therefore, no need to import the manufactures of outside barbarians in exchange for our own produce" (Perdue 2005; Berg 2006). Despite occasional expressions of dissent, the official view that China had anything much to learn from an augmented level of commercial intercourse with the west remained powerful even after another ignominious defeat by western powers in a second Opium war (Spence 1999). Retrospectively, the attitude aptly labelled by Mary Wright as "the last stand of Chinese Conservatism", has been explained, if not justified, by the longevity and success of an enormous and ecologically diverse empire that had been admired by Europeans since the sojourn of Marco Polo in the late thirteenth century (Wright 1957). That view had, moreover, persisted over more or less five hundred years of encounters and contacts between the occident and imperial China under the rule of its Mongol, Ming and Manchu dynasties (Barrow 1806; Dawson 1967).

Over these centuries connexions with Europeans took place, mainly in China and impressions of the empire were communicated to Europe in the form of commercial intelligence from merchants engaged in transcontinental trade with the east, in travelogues published by a tiny number of curious tourists and more elaborately as annual reports from the sixteenth century onwards, written by Christian missionaries, particularly Jesuits, who spent their lives and careers as foreign consultants to the Court in Beijing or, less comfortably, in futile endeavours to convert a mere fraction of the Chinese population to the values and rituals of Roman Catholicism (Mackerras 1989; Mungello 2005).

Europe's only other vista on Imperial China (again facilitated by its own merchants and ships) occurred indirectly through the import and consumption of tea and "Chinoiserie" that included such luxurious commodities as fine silks and cotton cloth, porcelain, pharmaceuticals, jewels and other exotic items. Thus, as late as the eighteenth century, western knowledge of China and that cultures impressive range of contributions to the world's technologies for navigation, written and printed forms of communication, agronomy, industry, transportation and the scientific comprehension of the natural world remained limited, impressionistic and confined by a preoccupation with differences in religious and moral values as well as concerns for prospects of profitable commerce (Temple 1998; Mote 1999; Spence 1999; Jones 2013).

Nevertheless, their limited knowledge about the "Middle Kingdom" did not deter a celebrated network of Europe's public intellectuals from representing China as a model of enlightenment for their own political, economic, social and religious elites to follow (Staunton 1853–54). Needless to say, the selective and laudatory representations of the empire's culture and institutions conveyed in publications by a long line of famous European intellectuals (including Bacon, Bayle, Bernier, Vauban, Voltaire,

## 1 HISTORIOGRAPHICAL CONTEXT AND BIBLIOGRAPHICAL GUIDE 5

Turgot, Quesnay and Leibniz) was not only offensive to Europe's aristocratic elites and Christian traditions, but contested by a range of moral philosophers, political economists and other intellectuals (including Montaigne, Montesquieu, Defoe, Hume, Diderot, d'Halbach, Helvitus, Smith and Malthus). They portrayed the Manchu state as despotic, its meritocratic bureaucracy as corrupt and China's potential for future scientific, technological and economic progress as exhausted. In the course of Europe's famous debate on Enlightenment, China's status was effectively degraded to a civilization in decline (Brook and Blue 1999). The more balanced and positive views of the empire's historical achievements in the spheres of politics, moral philosophy, culture, science, technology and economic management conveyed by the Jesuits (who had at least made serious attempts to comprehend another civilization) were more or less ignored (Maverick 1946; Mungello 2005).

By the time Lord Macartney's mission arrived in Beijing (where it was indeed treated with disdain by the Qianlong Emperor and his officials) intellectually the way had been prepared for a western view of the Chinese empire that was badly informed and primed to mature in a Eurocentric direction (Berg 2006).

Furthermore, the material foundations for the rise, strength and persistence of Europe's increasingly derogatory views of China (and India) were obviously locatable in the emergence, development and diffusion of a widening range of western technological innovations tenuously linked to advances in science maturing into institutionalized disciplines for the generation of systemic and reliable knowledge successfully applied to the problems of navigation, transportation, agriculture, mining, industry, commerce, bodily health and, above all, to geopolitical power (Black 2014; Sachsenmaier 2015).

Chinese deficiencies in all of these spheres (especially in weaponry, navigation and the development of scientific instruments) had been noted by Jesuits and foreign merchants over the eighteenth century. Following from displays of disinterest in the western knowledge and commodities brought to China by the Macartney mission, British and European commentaries on the scientific and technological and economic backwardness of the empire became sharper in tone, more common and comprehensive. They gradually widened from critiques of specified examples of the institutions to a derogation of Chinese civilization as a whole (Jones 2013).

6     P. K. O'BRIEN

As the nineteenth century progressed, the Qing state became less and less capable of defending the empire's territory and interests against British, French, Russian and Japanese naval and military power; and of maintaining internal order in the face of a sequence of destructive revolts and insurrections (Gernet 1982; Andrade 2016). Above all, that state failed to invest enough to prevent the depreciation of the empire's infrastructure of roads, waterways and facilities for irrigation and trade that underpinned an economy and society coping badly with unsustainable rates of population growth and the deepening of malign consequences that flowed from centuries of extensive and intensive economic growth based largely upon by environmental exploitation and depletion (Elvin 1973; Sierferle and Breuninger 2003).

Failures, by the Manchu state (1644–1911) to cope with the empire's heightened afflictions from deforestation, salination, floods and riverine silting as well as the need for infrastructural investment in its expanded territory for sedentary agriculture, threats to external security from the west, rapid population growth and serious interludes of internal disorder all operated to promote a tradition of European writing on both the condition of China and its status in world history that shifted radically over time from awe, through admiration to binary comparisons that covered a gamut of attitudes from compassion to racist contempt. All aspects of Chinese politics, society, culture, morals, religion, science and technology, as well as levels of economic development came under sustained and critical scrutiny from Western merchants, investors, diplomats, professional experts and missionaries to China (Cranmer-Byng 1962). Their views became more virulent when the Chinese rejected European advice and solutions to their problems in favour of a return to traditions that they perceived had served the empire well for nearly two millennia (Brook and Blue 1999).

As relative geopolitical and economic decline persisted, the political, moral and economic foundations of that tradition came into question, not only among Europeans, but also among a growing minority of China's educated elite, who favoured radical, institutional and cultural reform and became complicit in a western and derogatory discourse about their native culture and its history (Dixin and Chengming 2000).

In a climate dominated by the ideals of the French Revolution and the successes of capitalist imperialism, a line of European historical philosophers including Hegel, Fichte, Marx, Buckle, Spencer and Galton derogated the contributions and achievements to civilization of the world's largest and oldest empire which they represented as portraying despotism, legal confusion, moral and cultural stasis and a physiocratic attachment to peasant agriculture that was inimical to economic progress. Ironically for modern Maoists the most virulent of western critics, Marx, wrote in particularly scathing terms about the majority of the Chinese population, who for millennia had lived, worked and reproduced themselves in village communities which, in his words, "restrained the human mind within the smallest possible compass making it the unresisting tool of superstition, enslaving it beneath traditional rules and depriving it of all energy" (Frank 1998; Brook and Blue 1999).

By the nineteenth century for most Europeans the image of the Chinese empire and its history had moved on from an enlightened state ruling over an advanced and technologically progressive society to a despotism presiding over a stagnant economy and afflicted by decline and backwardness in almost all spheres of human endeavour (Dawson 1967).

Challenges to this hegemonic view emanated from Europeans who lived and worked in China as engineers, scientists, doctors, teachers, as well as missionaries. Many learned the language and studied the complexities and sophistication of this ancient civilization so that their writings betray only limited traces of the cultural chauvinism associated with the dominant western view of Imperial China. By 1914–1918 that view (based by then on Europe's unmistakeable superiority in science, technology and military power) had in any case been morally compromised by the barbarities of industrialized warfare among western powers.

Even before the Great War and the replacement of millennia of dynastic by republican rule in 1911, a reassessment began of China's culture and its long history of contributions to the world's moral philosophy, science, technology, medicine and agrarian development. That continued alongside the systematic search for the political, legal, institutional, social and economic reforms required to alleviate the new republic's omnipresent problems of internal order, external security, environmental degradation and industrial backwardness (Jones 2013).

Gradually in the writings of professional sinologists, sympathetic missionaries and philosophical historians such as Arnold Toynbee and H. G. Wells, Imperial China recovered some if its historical status as an enlightened despotism based upon the ancient and benign morality of Confucianism and presiding over a quasi-autonomous predominately agrarian society of commutarian villages. Famous social scientists such as

Buck, Hobson and Tawney also recognized the new republic's potential for economic development. Bertrand Russell who taught there in the 1920s found "among the nations of the world, China is quite peculiar because in population and potential strength Chinas is the greatest nation in the world, while in actual strength it is one of the least" (Jones 2013).

Max Weber who has exercised an enduring influence over all subsequent narratives by historians and investigations by social scientists into China's failure to develop economically, politically and culturally, engaged in a reciprocal and systematic exercise in comparisons with Western Europe in order to find an explanation for its relative decline (Vries 2013). Predictably perhaps Weber found it by drawing rather simplistic binary contrasts with his own prior analysis of the political, institutional, legal, cultural and above all, religious forces which, had over centuries of time promoted the emergence of successful industrial market economies within Western Europe (Elvin 1984).

From his Eurocentred perspective, Weber recognized, however, that capitalism and markets had been present in China since the Tang-Song dynasties (618–1279) but not in a form or with sufficient strength to overcome China's ancient and pervasive system of Confucian values. As Weber observed them, Chinese beliefs continued to sustain kinship-based institutions for agricultural and industrial production, an autocratic and patriarchal family system based upon a geist of obedience and duty producing a "strong attachment to the habitual" that constrained the spirit of individualism, rationality and private enterprise, which for Weberians explains the rise of the West (Weber 1951).

Weber's views on the Confucian foundations of the Chinese state and the institutions that its patrimonial bureaucracy sustained have been exposed as being even more contestable than his more famous thesis on "The Protestant Ethic and the Spirit of European Capitalism" (Elvin 1984; Bol 2008). Weberian endeavours to be systematically comparative have continued, however, to inform almost all scholarship designed to juxtapose and explain the rise of the West and the clear retardation and decline of China (Jones 1987). Most of the literature from comparative history and the social sciences that has appeared since Weber published in the 1920s has, however, matured to become less inclined to reify the cultural, religious and ideological contrasts between Occidental and Oriental societies and economies (Lieberman 2009; Broadberry and O'Rourke 2010; Prak and Van Zanden 2013; Vries 2013).

Historians of China have concentrated instead on the restoration of China to a place of prominence and significance in the writing of world histories that break with the gamut of Eurocentred assumptions that begin and end with the rise of the West (Fairbank 1978). Furthermore, historical perspectives derived from longer chronologies have exposed the empire's impressive record of governance that provided for tolerable levels of external security, internal order and standards of living for a large population settled in villages across an extensive territory containing a diverse range of environments (Feuerwerker 1992; Adshead 1995; Von Glahn 2016). Needham's multi-volume project on Science and Civilization in China has revealed an early, but extraordinary range of contributions to science, technology and moral philosophy. Chinese foods, medicines, manufactured commodities, modes of transport and forms of communication that flowed to the West over the centuries-long before Europeans confronted the Chinese with their own distinctive and superior range of useful knowledge of machinery, artefacts and desirable commodities, along with threats to the empire's security, stability and traditional way of life based upon an economy dominated by agriculture and household forms of production (Needham 1969, 1970).

Thus the lack of foresight, tardiness and resistance to structural and political change that marked the empire's response to the geopolitical and economic challenges posed by the rise of the West has prompted historians to survey narratives, analyses and debates that go back to the Enlightenment. They have recovered a library of publications which became increasingly critical of the Empire, which vary from Eurocentric impressionism through to the contemptuous Marxist and Liberal Fundamentalism embodied in such concepts as Asiatic modes of production and Oriental Despotism (Hobson 2004). Until very recent times economists, political scientists, sociologists and other academics engaged in the ongoing discourse about transitions to modernity have generally taken a negative (Weberian) stance towards the ideals and injunctions embodied in so-called "dead hand" of Confucianism which has continued to influence the strategies, policies and attitudes that China and the Chinese display towards the modernization of their culture even under its communist regime (Ferguson 2011; Duchesne 2011).

Meanwhile, among historians with the linguistic credentials and range of knowledge to conduct the research required to contextualize and evaluate the response of Ming and Qing China to challenges posed by the geopolitical and economic rise of the West, there is now a broad recognition that between, say 1492 and 1815, both the Orient and Occident entered into "the transition to modernity with different combinations of assets and liabilities" (Brook 2011). Among those liabilities (elaborated decades ago in Mark Elvin's classical analytical narrative) are several that reveal how a precocious start and centuries of success as an organic economy led to a peak of production possibilities or a "high level equilibrium trap" (Elvin 1973, 1996). Such penalties from early starts are commonplace in histories of economic development (Wood 2002). Latterly the widespread revival of concerns with the environment has, moreover, reconfigured the long-term economic consequences that flow from the protracted and increasingly intensive exploitation of natural resources and unavoidable degradation of local ecologies for Europe as well as China (Marks 1998, 2012; Pomeranz 2000).

Histories of connexions and comparisons between China and Europe have currently reached the most recent phase of a protracted discourse with antecedents that go back to Marco Polo, which has acquired the evocative title of the Great Divergence Debate. That debate was precipitated by four seminal books published around the turn of the millennium by Roy Bin Wong, "China Transformed. Historical Change and the Limits of European Experience" (1997), David Landes, "The Wealth and Poverty of Nations". "Why Some are So Rich and Some are So Poor?" (1998); Andre Gunder Frank, "ReOrient, Global Economy in the Asian Age" (1998) and Ken Pomeranz, "The Great Divergence, China, Europe and the Making of the Modern World Economy" (2000). The Landes book (anticipated by Eric Jones, "European Miracle" (1981) can be clearly situated in a Eurocentric tradition of writing about the Chinese empire. While the books by Bin Wong, Frank and Pomeranz, designed to rescue China from the condescensions of that tradition, reflect a mood in contemporary sinology that had been eloquently expressed as early as 1984 by Paul Cohen's book, "Discovering History in China". *American Historical Writings on the Recent Past*. Cohen vigorously asserted that "the assumption of China as incapable of self-generating change requiring for its transformation a force without, that in the wake of western intrusion, traditional Chinese society would give way to a new modern China fashioned in the image of the West, this whole structure of assumptions is thoroughly shaken" (Cohen 1984).

My short text for the Palgrave Pivot series has been designed to investigate just how far the basis for modern western assumptions about Imperial

China has been shaken out of the fetters of Eurocentred views of the empire's economic development by protagonists and their opponents in the course of intellectually stimulating and ongoing debate surrounding the Great Divergence between economies (and by dubious extension to "civilizations") at the western and eastern ends of Eurasia (Hobson 2004; Duchesne 2011; Ferguson, 2011).

That challenge (inspired by the recent return to environmental history) has proceeded on several fronts and confronts an established view that for some three to four centuries only European history could be retrospectively represented as exemplifying elements of a progressive trajectory for the construction of states, the formation of institutions, the extension of markets for domestic and overseas trade, the consolidation of cultures for enterprise and above all, the discovery and diffusion of a range of scientific, technological and organizational innovations required for transitions to modern economic growth (Braudel 1981–84; Bairoch 1998; Landes 1998; Broadberry and O'Rourke 2010; Broadberry 2018).

Historians with credentials and expertise in Chinese history have rejected claims that all these elements for a trajectory towards a plateau of possibilities of sustained increases in the productivity of labour and rising standards for living were quintessentially occidental. They insist they had antecedents in the Orient and continued, moreover, to operate more or less efficiently in China (as well as Japan and India) until surprisingly late in the eighteenth century (Wong 1997; Frank 1998; Pomeranz 2000; Von Glahn 2016; Francks 2016).

Furthermore, they have extended their critique to make a secondary but strategic point in this debate, namely that European historiography has continued to downplay singular and significant advantages that Britain and other mainland economies had derived from favourable natural endowments (particularly coal), as well as the enormous bounty derived from imports of arboreal products, foodstuffs, organic raw materials, bullion and minerals that flowed from the fortuitous discovery and colonization of the Americas as well as the exploitative gains derived from servicing trade between the Occident and Orient (Frank 1998; Waley-Cohen 1999; Goldstone 2008; Goody 2010; Marks 2016).

Predictably all these Sinocentred claims have been contested point by point by European and American historians and economists. They continue to produce historical evidence much of it in the form of statistics purporting to represent the specificities and superiorities of Europe's states, institutions, overseas commerce, cultures and, above all,

12 P. K. O'BRIEN

its advanced technologies that generated and sustained higher levels of productivity and standards of living (Acemoglu and Robinson 2013). Although most scholars engaged with comparative global history have been compelled to recognize that for some centuries before and after the discovery of the Americas, China could be plausibly ranked as the most advanced organic economy in the world (Daly 2015; Deng 2016).

## REFERENCES

Acemoglu, D., & Robinson, J. (2013). *Why nations fail: The origins of power, prosperity and poverty*. New York: Crown Publishers.

Andrade, T. (2016). *The gunpowder age: China's military innovation and the rise of the west in world history*. Princeton: Princeton University Press.

Adshead, S. (1995). *China in world history*. London: Palgrave Macmillan.

*American Historical Review Forum*. (2002). Political economy and ecology on the eve of industrialization: Europe, China and the global conjuncture. *107*(2).

Bairoch, P. (1998). *Victoires et déboires. Histoire economique et sociale du monde du XVI$^e$ siècle à nos jours*. 2 vols. Paris: Gallimard.

Barrow, J. (1806). *Travels in China containing descriptions, observations and comparisons*. London: T. Cadell and W. Davies.

Black, J. (2014). *The power of knowledge: How information technology made the modern world*. New Haven: Yale University Press.

Berg, M. (2006). British industry and perceptions of China: Mathew Boulton, useful knowledge and the McCartney Embassy to China, 1792–94. *Journal of Global History, 1,* 269–288.

Bol, P. (2008). *Neo-confucianism in history*. Cambridge, MA: Harvard University Press.

Braudel, F. (1981–84). *Civilization and capitalism*. 3 vols. London: University of California Press.

Broadberry, S., Hanhui, G., & David, D. L. (2018). China, Europe and the great divergence: A study in historical national accounting. *Journal of Economic History, 78,* 1–46.

Broadberry, S., & O'Rourke, K. (2010). *The Cambridge economic history of modern Europe: Vol. 1. 1700–1800*. Cambridge: Cambridge University Press.

Brook, T. (2011). *The Troubled Empire: China in the Yuan and Ming dynasties*. Cambridge: Harvard University Press.

Brook, T., & Blue, G. (Eds.). (1999). *China and historical capitalism*. Cambridge: Cambridge University Press.

*Canadian Journal of Sociology*. (2008). *33*(1).

# 1 HISTORIOGRAPHICAL CONTEXT AND BIBLIOGRAPHICAL GUIDE   13

Cohen, P. (1984). *Discovering history in China: American historical writing on the recent Chinese past*. New York: Columbia University Press.

Cranmer-Byng, J. (Ed.). (1962). *An embassy to China: Lord Macartney's Journal*. London: Longmans, Green & Co.

Daly, J. (2015). *Historians debate the rise of the West*. Abingdon: Routledge.

Dawson, R. (1967). *The Chinese chameleon: An analysis of European conceptions of China*. Oxford: Oxford University Press.

Deng, K. (2016). *Mapping China's growth and development in the long run, 221 BC to 2020*. Singapore: World Scientific Publishing Company.

Dixin, X., & Chengming, W. (Eds.). (2000). *Chinese capitalism 1522–1840*. London: Palgrave Macmillan.

Duchesne, R. (2011). *The uniqueness of western civilization*. Leiden: Brill.

Eckstein, A. (1968). *Economic trends in communist China*. Chicago: University of Chicago Press.

Eichengreen, B., Gupta, P., & Kumar, R. (Eds). (2010). *Emerging giants: China and India in the world economy*. Cambridge: Cambridge University Press.

Elvin, M. (1973). *The pattern of the Chinese past*. Stanford: Stanford University Press.

Elvin, M. (1984). Why China failed to create an endogenous capitalism? A critique of Weber's explanation. *Theory and Society, 13*, 379–391.

Elvin, M. (1996). *Another history: Essays on China from a European perspective*. Honolulu: University of Hawaii Press.

Fairbank, J. (Ed.). (1978). *Cambridge history of China*. Cambridge: Cambridge University Press.

Ferguson, N. (2011). *Civilization: The west and the rest*. London: Allen Lane.

Feuerwerker, A. (1992). *Studies in the economics of late imperial China*. Ann Arbor: Michigan University Press.

Francks, P. (2016). *Japan and the great divergence*. London: Palgrave Macmillan.

Frank, A. G. (1998). *ReOrient. Global economy in the Asian age*. London: University of California Press.

Gernet, J. (1982). *A history of Chinese civilization*. Cambridge: Cambridge University Press.

Goldstone, J. (2008). *Why Europe? The rise of the west in world history 1500–1850*. New York: McGraw Hill.

Goody, J. (2010). *The Eurasian miracle*. Cambridge: Cambridge University Press.

Grinin, L., & Korotayev, A. (2015). *Great divergence and great convergence*. Cham: Springer.

Hobson, J. (2004). *The eastern origins of western civilization*. Cambridge: Cambridge University Press.

Jones, D. (2013). *The image of China in western social and political thought*. Houndsmills: Palgrave Macmillan.

Jones, E. (1987). *The European miracle. Environments, economies and geopolitics in the history of Europe and Asia*. Cambridge: Cambridge University Press.

*Journal of Asian Studies*. (2002). *61*(2).

*Journal of Asian Studies*. (2003). *62*(1).

Landes, D. (1998). *The wealth and poverty of nations*. London: Little Brown and Co.

Lieberman, V. (2009). Strange parallels: South-East Asia in global context, c. 800–1830. Vol. II, *Mainland Mirrors: Europe, Japan, China, South Asia and the islands*. Cambridge, MA: Harvard University Press.

Mackerras, C. (1989). *Western images of China*. Oxford: Oxford University Press.

Marks, R. (1998). *Tigers, rice, silk and silt: Environment and economy in Late Imperial South China*. Cambridge: Cambridge University Press.

Marks, R. (2012). *China: Its environment and its history*. New York: Rowman & Littlefield.

Marks, S. (2016). *Global capitalism from the renaissance to the present*. Cambridge: Cambridge University Press.

Maverick, L. (1946). *China: A model for Europe*. San Antonio: Paul Anderson Company.

Mote, F. (1999). *Imperial China 900–1800*. Cambridge, MA: Harvard University Press.

Mungello, D. (2005). *The great encounter of China and the west*. Lanham: Rowman & Littlefield.

Needham, J. (1969). *The great titration: Science and society in east and west*. Toronto: University of Toronto Press.

Needham, J. (1970). *Clerks and craftsmen in China and the west*. Cambridge: Cambridge University Press.

Parthasarathi, P. (2010). *Why Europe grew rich and Asia did not: Global economic divergence, 1600–1850*. Cambridge: Cambridge University Press.

Perdue, P. (2005). *China marches west: The Qing conquest of Central Asia*. London: Belknap Press of Harvard University Press.

Perez, M., & De Sousa, L. (2018). *History and polycentric approaches*. Singapore: World Scientific Publishing.

Phillips, J. (1998). *The medieval expansion of Europe*. Oxford: Oxford University Press.

Pomeranz, K. (2000). *The great divergence: China, Europe and the making of the modern world economy*. Princeton: Princeton University Press.

Prak, M., & Van Zanden, J.-L. (2013). *Technology skills and the pre-modern economy in the west and east*. Leiden: Brill.

Ringmar, E. (2007). *Why Europe was first? Social and economic growth in Europe and East Asia, 1500–1850*. New York: Anthem Press.

Sachsenmaier, D. (2015). Chinese definitions of the European—Some historical examples. *Comparative 25*.

Sierferle, R., & Breuninger, H. (Eds.). (2003). *Agriculture, population and development in China and Europe.* Stuttgart: Breuninger Stiftung GmbH.

Spence, J. (1999). *The Chan's great continent. China in western minds.* New York: W.W. Norton.

Staunton, G. (Ed.). (1853). *Juan Mendoza's: The history of the great and mighty kingdom of China.* 2 Vols. London: Hakluyt Society.

Temple, R. (1998). *The genius of China: 3000 years of science, discovery and invention.* London: Prion Books.

Von Glahn, R. (2016). *The economic history of China from antiquity to the nineteenth century.* Cambridge: Cambridge University Press.

Vries, P. (2013). *Escaping poverty: The origins of modern economic growth.* Vienna: V & R unipress/Vienna University Press.

Vries, P. (2015). *State economy and the great divergence: Great Britain and China 1680s–1850s.* London: Bloomsbury.

Vries, P. (2020). *Averting the great divergence. State and economy in Japan, 1868– 37.* London: Bloomsbury Academic.

Waley-Cohen, J. (1999). *The sextants of Beijing. Global currents in Chinese history.* New York: W.W. Norton.

Weber, M. (1951). *The religion of China.* Glencoe: The Free Press.

Wong, R. B. (1997). *China transformed: Historical change and the limits of European experience.* Ithaca: Cornell University Press.

Wood, E. (2002). *The origins of capitalism—A longer view.* New York: Verso.

Wright, M. (1957). *The last stand of Chinese conservationism.* Stanford: Stanford University Press.

CHAPTER 2

# Statistical Bases for a Chronology of Economic Divergence Between Imperial China and Western Europe, 1638–1839

**Abstract** This chapter evaluates the data used, defined and disputed by scholars engaged in providing a statistically based chronology for divergence in order to "test" the key revisionist proposition, namely, that for centuries before the Industrial Revolution, the standards of productivity and welfare afforded by the economies of China and Western Europe for their populations were surprisingly similar. If this extensively and intensely disputed "fact" turns out to be plausible, then claims for the superiority of Europe's historical trajectories for the evolution of more effective states, economic institutions, cultural beliefs and systems for the accumulation of useful knowledge would be undermined. Predictably western economic historians have subjected this core thesis of the California School to the tests that their discipline recommends to measure rates and levels of welfare provided by national economies for their populations. They claim to have "demonstrated" that per capita outputs, heights and incomes from real wages were measurable, discernible and different long before the late eighteenth century. Under close scrutiny the volume and quality of historical data available (particularly for Imperial China) is (for conceptual as well as factual reasons) not fit for the purpose of providing a statistically based chronology for divergence. The numbers in print even when they look congruent with qualitative historical evidence have remained (over a protracted period of dispute)

© The Author(s), under exclusive license to Springer Nature Switzerland AG 2020
P. K. O'Brien, *The Economies of Imperial China and Western Europe*, Palgrave Studies in Economic History, https://doi.org/10.1007/978-3-030-54614-4_2

conceptually ambiguous, statistically invalid and unacceptable as historical evidence for the plausible conjectures required to simultaneously measure changes over time for Imperial China and for contemporaneous comparisons with Western European economies. For both sides of the debate the laudable endeavours to quantify the quantifiable can be represented as a misplaced paradigm for historical research because it depends on more plausible bodies of data to trace, track and explain divergence over time.

**Keywords** Historical trajectories · Retardation · Stasis · Kuznetian paradigm · GDP · Maddison · Broadberry · Deng · Index numbers · Real wages · Standards of living · Organic economy · Productivity

After twenty-odd years of lively debate, analyses of the Great Divergence might now plausibly begin with a recognition that in all probability for at least 1500 years CE the organic economy of imperial China may be represented as being economically and technologically more advanced than the cluster of national economies that are located within the frontiers of modern western Europe. Only late in the day did that interconnected group of countries evolve to become scientifically, technically, economically and geopolitically the most developed and powerful in the world (Goldstone 2002, 2008; Hobson 2004; Lieberman 2009; Goody 2010; Daly 2014).

Thus the modern Divergence Debate has concentrated on the meta question of when, how and why the national economies of Western Europe led by Britain became clearly more advanced than the economy of Imperial China (Baumol 1994; Goldstone 2008). Since these two regions of Eurasia had remained in economic terms virtually disconnected economically for centuries preceding divergence, analytical comparisons in modern global history could refer to but more or less, neglect interconnexions and concentrate on two contrasting trajectories for economic growth (Gregory 2003; MacFarlane 2014; Vries 2015; Roy and Riello 2019).

The core question is why one historical trajectory led to the observed and more rapid development of western economies, while for some three or four centuries before the French and Industrial Revolutions the other exhibited nothing better than a trend of pronounced retardation and decline. Either way, and within a world economy of increasingly extensive and intensive geopolitical and economic connexions (including commerce and competition between Europe and Asia) most historians agree that the relative position of China deteriorated (Marks 2016). The empire's retardation has been explained with reference to the maintenance of a traditional political system, for the governance of a vast territorial empire, archaic institutions, conservative beliefs and backward technology which for centuries had placed and continued to maintain China's agrarian economy upon a trajectory leading to avoidable stasis and a prolonged widening of divergence with Europe, North America and Australasia (Lebow et al. 2006; Ringmar 2007; MacFarlane 2014).

The core of the modern revisionist rejection of this view (which has provoked a vigorous counterattack) can be read in the writings of the California School. That School has formulated, fortified and defended a now famous thesis that maintains that for centuries before the French Revolution, the economies of Western Europe and China operated in ways and at levels of efficiency that look surprisingly similar. Furthermore, before that time the supposedly superior political systems, cultural beliefs, economic institutions and technologies of Western European nations had not generated anything approximating to the clear differentials in the productivities and standards of living for their populations that are regarded as the hallmarks of more advanced and progressive economic systems (Pomeranz 2000).

Thus the dispute over a chronology for contrasts in per capita levels of welfare provided by the Chinese economy for its population compared to European standards, forms an essential preface to any serious discourse about convergence and divergence (Baumol 1994). Acceptable statistics are required to test the plausibility of revisionist arguments deployed by the California School to undermine the established Euro-centred/Weberian view. Namely that divergence occurred because the frameworks of: cultural beliefs, legal regulations and political institutions surrounding production in Imperial China operated in ways that were not promotional for modern economic grouth (Goldstone 2008; Parthasarathi 2010; Von Glahn 2016; Roy and Riello 2019).

Western economists and economic historians have not been slow to respond to the challenge to provide both theoretically plausible reasons as well as more dubious and contentious statistical evidence to undermine the critique that their views of late Imperial China are superficial and

Eurocentric. Predictably they continue to subject core theses of the California School to the heavy artillery of standard and familiar tests deployed by economists and economic historians to quantify rates of growth and relative levels of welfare provided by national economies for their citizens (Kuznets 1966; Maddison 2007; Broadberry et al. 2018).

This programme of historical research has been central for the divergence debate and continues to uncover statistical evidence that has been heuristic to contemplate, compare and elaborate upon as ways of understanding the economic histories of both pre-modern Imperial China and Western Europe. It has matured into a major example of the paradigm established decades ago by for the study of national economic histories, empirical economics and the application of comparative methods for global histories of long-term economic growth by a Nobel Prize winner in Economics, Simon Kuznets (Kuznets 1971; vide Floud et al. *Cambridge Economic Histories of Britain*, Vol. 1, editions for 1981, 1994, 2004 and 2014; Broadberry and O'Rourke 2010; Fogel et al. 2013).

Unfortunately, the plausibility of the results flowing from this potentially productive paradigm for historical research to generate quantified conjectures about the relative levels as well as the rates, patterns and mechanisms for the long-term economic development of firms, farms, towns, regions, countries and empires depends upon: the availability, accessibility, volume and quantity of statistical evidence as well as the care taken by scholars engaged with the construction of Kuznetian indices (Fogel et al. 2013). Such indices have been designed to measure and compare, for example, relative levels of GDP per capita and real wage rates for Europe's skilled and unskilled labourers with family incomes for modal Chinese peasants. Given the prestige that modern economics and economic history attaches to quantification as analogous to a scientific method for the validation of historical evidence *prima facie*, the construction of this hard-won and transparent body of statistical evidence has ostensibly undermined the claims of the California School by revealing that the measured contrasts in productivity between the economies of late Imperial China and Western Europe appear in the data well before the late eighteenth century. Divergence could, therefore, continue to be analysed and explained with reference to long-term deficiencies in the cultures and institutions for the management of Imperial China's organic economy (Van Zanden and Ma 2017; Broadberry et al. 2018).

Chronology remains central to the argument that Europeans and Chinese lived and worked in a world of "surprising resemblances" until late in the eighteenth century because if that periodization could be supported by hard statistical evidence, then the long-run defects (posited by Weberians) in the culture, institutions and above all in the constitution of the state established and maintained over the millennia for the management of a very large imperial economy would no longer remain tenable (Deng and O'Brien 2017). Furthermore, an acceptable statistical chronology for Europe's convergence towards and ultimate divergence from China could then be more plausibly represented from a Sinocentred perspective as the outcome of a range of fortuitous and contingent factors including: Europe's natural endowment of a known underexploited but eventually highly significant source of energy, namely coal; the discovery and exploitation of a truly massive bounty of natural resources in the Americas; and the unintended consequences of interstate rivalry, mercantilist competition and protracted interludes of warfare that flowed from Europe's failure to construct and sustain a single hegemonic state to rule and regulate that subcontinent (Lebow et al. 2006 and special issues of *Canadian Journal of Sociology* 2004, 2008; *Economic History Review* 2011; Vries 2015).

A brigade of distinguished scholars with credentials in European economic history aided and abetted by a platoon of economists educated at western universities have continued to maintain that their properly calibrated data sets demonstrate that divergence was occurring much earlier than the eighteenth century (Maddison 2007; Broadberry et al. 2018). If that is the case, then the recently gathered and calibrated statistical evidence supports traditional Eurocentred views that the locus, origins and the persistence of the relative backwardness of Imperial China can be found (as Weberians suggest) in the cultural beliefs and in the political, legal and institutional frameworks established for production that were in place and operative long before a clear conjuncture of divergence emerged and widened over the nineteenth and twentieth centuries (Jones 1987; Wood 2002; Ringmar 2007; Howell 2010).

Unfortunately, the statistics utilized by both sides in this debate won't wash (Feuerwerker 1973; Vanhaute [ed.], *Special Issue of Low Countries Journal of Social and Economic History* 2015) As most historians in touch with the primary sources utilized for macro-economic measurement recognize even for western European economies (with archives of official data for the construction of indices that are reliable) plausible conjectures for rates and relative levels of economic development have been difficult to construct and on close examination often turn out to be less than durable (Perrson 2010; Bateman 2012; Vries 2015). For Imperial China, even the most basic evidence required for the construction of plausible conjectures for such macro-economic indices as total population, the areas of land cultivated and cropped, nominal wage rates, outputs of major crops and industrial commodities, exports and imports, standardized or standardizable money of account are simply not available (Howell 2010; Feuerwerker 1973; Kuroda 2013; Deng and O'Brien 2015, 2016). But for a contentious rebuttal of this view read the articles by Van Zanden and Ma and the reply by Deng and O'Brien (Van Zanden and Ma 2017; Deng and O'Brien 2017 reply in the same journal).

Recent and forensic investigations into the data utilized by both sides in the Divergence Debate have, therefore, reluctantly concluded that the application of the Kuznetsian paradigm for historical research designed to locate the conjuncture in premodern history when divergence emerged, persisted and widened is not viable (Deng and O'Brien 2016). As Imre Lakatos might have said for this particular debate, the paradigm is degenerate. Its status approximates to conceptual art in the history of art and as such is convincing to those who accept the impressions conveyed by their constructed numbers as historical facts that approximate to the explicanda required for analytical narratives of long-run growth.

For readers of this short introduction to a great debate on divergence, it could be tedious to engage in detail with an important but voluminous subsection of recently published literature concerned to establish conceptually valid and statistically acceptable indices that might serve to locate an historical chronology for convergence and divergence between the late imperial economy of China and a cluster of national economies located in Western Europe. For debates on the availability of statistical data readers should consult the dispute between Van Zanden and Ma and Deng and O'Brien in World Economics (Deng and O'Brien 2017).

Exercises designed to produce indicators for purposes of comparisons in economic history are commonplace and are predicated on two definitions. The first seeks to specify the explicanda or what a particular index seeks to convey. Participants in this debate offer indices that purport to measure relative levels and changes over time in averaged standards of welfare afforded by the economies of late imperial China and Western Europe to their respective populations. Given differences in the size of those populations, areas of territory and regional variations in standards of living across these two extensive geographical entities, many publications in the debate have followed suggestions from Pomeranz to concentrate upon the most commercialized and economically advanced regions of Western Europe and China. His sensible suggestion has left publications on England and the Netherlands to represent Western Europe and the provinces surrounding Lake Tai in the Yangtze Delta, three major cities (Beijing, Canton and Suzhou) and one tiny prefecture (Songjiang) to somehow represent the Chinese empire (Li and Van Zanden 2012; Hatcher and Stephenson 2018).

Clearly narrowing geographical and social spaces for purposes of conducting comparisons in "global" economic history is neither satisfactory or satisfying and may account for the predilection among economists who have engaged with this debate to continue with, and to refine, a series of estimates for gross domestic products per capita, calibrated in a common numeraire of 1990 international dollars by the late Angus Maddison that purport to refer to the whole of China (Maddison 2007; Broadberry et al. 2018; but see de Jong and Van Ark 2012).

Maddison's transparent endeavours and their recent refinements designed to provide estimates for the best of all possible numbers for international comparisons for rates of change and relative levels of social welfare, namely figures for gross domestic products per capita remain heuristic to contemplate (Broadberry et al. 2018). Nevertheless, they are deeply flawed and for reasons that have been widely debated among economists and by historians, with the credentials required to appraise the properties of index numbers as well as the range and quality of primary sources available for the construction of macro-economic estimates for the levels of commodity and service outputs produced in Ming and Qing China (Deng and O'Brien 2017). The numbers in print remain conceptually ambiguous, statistically invalid and unacceptable as standard historical evidence for "plausible conjectures" (Bolt and Van Zanden 2018; Deng and O'Brien 2021). Nevertheless, debate on the feasibility of simultaneously measuring changes overtime in levels of domestic production for late Imperial China and for conducting contemporaneous comparisons with Western European economies continues and is unlikely to end any time soon (Deaton and Heston 2010; Stiglitz et al. 2010; Deng and O'Brien 2016, 2017; Brunt 2019; Goldstone 2019; but vide Van Zanden and Ma 2017).

Less ambitious and programmes of historical research designed to construct a foundational chronology and statistical framework for a focussed analysis of divergence based upon data for real wages are again heuristic to contemplate and discuss (Broadberry and Gupta 2006). They are also, alas, conceptually flawed and are not statistically viable for comparisons with late Imperial China (Allen et al. 2005, 2011; Deng and O'Brien 2015, 2016; Hatcher and Stephenson 2018).

For such comparisons within Europe, sources recording runs of real daily wage rates offered to skilled and unskilled labour employed by urban construction industries have, however, served as acceptable proxies or plausible conjectures for relative standards of living across advanced western economies. Unfortunately (as the team of scholars involved in a project to include China candidly admit) the data available for Chinese nominal wage rates has been difficult to accumulate on a scale sufficient to become accepted as a representative sample of quotations that could conceivably refer to the Chinese workforce as a whole. (Allen et al. 2005, 2011; Deng and O'Brien 2016). Most of the statistics for wage rates currently in print refer to wages paid on scales established by the state, fail to record commonplace and significant payments in kind and are denominated in taels of silver which is a unit of monetary account exchanged for locally variable amounts of wen—the currency used by wage dependent families to purchase the goods and services that they consumed (Kuroda 2013). Records that refer to daily rates of pay received by both skilled and unskilled labourers in late Imperial China are not commensurable with ostensibly comparable historical evidence for Western Europe where: much higher proportions of the workforce depended upon waged labour for its standard of living; payments in kind were less common; records usually refer to currencies utilized by workers and their families for day-to-day purchases in local markets. European workers were detached from access to cultivable land and from opportunities to work in kin-based households and networks for production. Unless and until the meanings and inferences that might be drawn from Chinese (and Indian?) records for nominal wage rates are clarified as comparable they will remain far too ambiguous as evidence for the construction of plausible indicators for relative standards of living afflicting wage dependent families in late Imperial China, India and even for most of Europe before, say 1850 (Deng and O'Brien 2015; Hatcher and Stephenson 2018).

The challenge is not to find data that is more or less commensurable with European data, but to focus on social groups where standards of living and welfare might be measured in ways that could arguably be represented as a proxy of just how well the economies of Europe and China may have catered for the material welfare of their populations before, during and after the Great Divergence (Allen et al. 2005; Deng and O'Brien 2015).

Perhaps the sole way of arriving at a proxy that might help to locate a chronology for divergence is to accept the obvious fact that by the seventeenth century the two workforces were becoming less and less commensurable (Rawski and Li 1992). Even in the most advanced and prosperous regions of the empire a majority of Chinese workers retained access to land and produced food, organic raw materials and manufactured commodities within a framework of institutions dominated by households or kin-based units for production (Perkins 1969; So 2013). That was not the case for the more advanced, urban and prosperous towns and regions of Western Europe (Brenner and Isett 2002). Thus, one potentially meaningful method of dating outcomes that flowed from this ostensibly significant contrast is (as Mark Elvin, recognized decades ago) would be to compare peasant households engaged in a combination of agrarian and industrial production with the real incomes of European families dependent on wages from employment in industry and services located in towns. Even that way to circumvent the impasse may not, however, be possible because as a recently published dispute over official statistics for the size of farms cultivated in the Yangtze Delta between Pomeranz and his critics shows the validity of the exercise hinges on whether the modal area under cultivation around 1750 was 7.5 or 10.5 mu? The latter figure if it could the validated, would lend strong statistically-based support for the California Schools core hypothesis that divergence may have appeared too late to support Weberian views that the scale, governance, institutions and culture of the Chinese economy had evolved historically on a path-dependent trajectory leading to divergence with the West (Deng and O'Brien 2015).

It is certainly regrettable that this core hypothesis cannot be tested statistically. Nevertheless, the assumption maintained by scholars on both sides of the divergence debate that China's imperial centralized state rationally managed by a meritocratic bureaucracy assessed and collected the range of reliable statistics required for the economic and social governance of a vast and diverse territory with a large population (and its locally and lightly governed empire) was not held by previous generations of historians of China (Naquin and Rawski 1987; Feuerwerker 1992; Leonard and Watt 1992). Sinologists are, moreover, aware that the records of dynasties before the Qing were destroyed after their official histories had been written up in classical Chinese—a linguistic credential that is not widespread even among Chinese historians (Dunstan 1996; Deng 2012; Shi 2018).

Thus the credence placed in the course of this famous debate on the primary sources available for a Kuznetsian analysis of the economic history of the Ming and Qing empires is in large part unwarranted. For both sides of the debate it represents a misplaced deployment of a paradigm that depends on more plausible bodies of statistical evidence (Brandt and Rawski 2008; Rowe 2009).

The eminent sinologist, Richard Von Glahn, has recently observed: "In recent years research into and analysis into quantitative history has often been based on fragmented historical data collected from Chinese literature. One big problem is that European scholars lack both the knowledge and theoretical structure of China's economic history and therefore are unable to evaluate the quality of the quantitative data that they use" (From a lecture delivered by Richard Von Glahn at Peking University in May 2019, as translated by Kent Deng). Vide Deng and O'Brien, Critical Survey (2021) of official and secondary sources available for the economics of divergence 1650–1850 (cited in Chapter 7).

## REFERENCES

Allen, R. C., Bengtsson, T., & Dribe, M. (2005). *Living standards in the past. New perspectives on well- being in Asia and Europe.* Oxford: Oxford University Press.

Allen, R. C., Bassino, J. P., Ma, D., Moll-Murata, C., & van Zanden, J.-L. (2011). Wages, prices and living standards in China in comparison with Europe, Japan and India. *Economic History Review, 64,* 8–38.

Bateman, V. (2012). *Markets and growth in early modern Europe.* London: Routledge.

Baumol, W. (1994). *Convergence of productivity: Cross national studies and historical evidence.* Oxford: Oxford University Press.

Bolt, J., & Van Zanden, J-L. (2018). Rebasing Maddison. *Maddison Project Working Paper 10.* University of Groningen Growth and Development Center.

Brandt, L., & Rawski, T. (Eds.). (2008). *China's great transformation.* Cambridge: Cambridge University Press.

Brenner, R., & Isett, C. (2002). England's divergence from China's Yangtze delta: Property relations, microeconomics and patterns of development. *Journal of Asian Studies, 61,* 609–662.

Broadberry, S., & Gupta, B. (2006). The early modern great divergence: Wages, prices and economic development in Europe and Asia, 1500–1800. *Economic History Review, 59,* 2–31.

Broadberry, S., & O'Rourke, K. (2010) *The Cambridge Economic History of Modern Europe. Vol. 1: 1700–1800.* Cambridge, MA: Cambridge University Press.

Broadberry, S., Guan, H., & Li, D. (2018). China, Europe and the great divergence. A study in historical national accounting. *Journal of Economic History, 78,* 955–1000.

Brunt, L. (2019). *Why international Geary Khamis Dollars cannot be a foundation for long run comparisons on GDP.* Unpublished paper, Norwegian School of Economics.

*Canadian Journal of Sociology.* (2004).

*Canadian Journal of Sociology.* (2008).

Daly, J. (2014). *Historians debate the rise of the west.* Abingdon: Routledge.

Deaton, A., & Heston, A. (2010). Understanding purchasing power parities and purchasing power parity national accounts. *American Journal of Macroeconomics, 2,* 4.

de Jong, H., & van Ark, B. (2012). *The comparison of GDP levels in the use of PPP's in the Maddison data base.* Working Paper Groningen Growth and Development Center.

Deng, K. (2012). *China's political economy in Modern Times: Changes and economic consequences 1800–2000.* Abingdon: Routledge.

Deng, K., & O'Brien, P. (2015). Nutritional standards of living in England and the Yangtze Delta Area circa 1644–circa 1840. *Journal of World History, 26*(2), 233–267.

Deng, K., & O'Brien, P. (2016). Establishing statistical foundations for the great divergence: A survey and critique of relative wage levels for Ming-Qing China. *Economic History Review, 69*(4), 1057–1082.

Deng, K., & O'Brien, P. (2017). How far back in time might macro-economic facts travel? The debate on the great divergence between imperial China and the west. *World Economics, 18,* 2.

Deng, K., & O'Brien, P. (2021). The Kuznetsian Paradigm and the Study of Global Economic History. Department of Economic History, London School of Economics. Working Paper 321.

Dunstan, H. (1996). *Conflicting counsels to confuse the age: A documentary history of the political economy of Qing China.* Ann Arbor: Michigan University Press.

*Economic History Review.* (2011). 6, 4.

Feuerwerker, A. (1973). Questions about China's early modern history that I wish I could answer. *Journal of Asian Studies, 51*(4), 757–769.

Feuerwerker, A. (1992). *Studies in the economic history of late imperial China.* Ann Arbor: Michigan University Press.

Floud, R. et al. (Edns.1981, 1994, 2004, 2014). *Cambridge Economic Histories of Britain*. Vol. 1.

Fogel, R., Fogel, E. M., Guglielmo, M., & Grotte, N. (2013). *Political arithmetic: Simon Kuznets and the empirical tradition in economics*. Chicago: Chicago University Press.

Goldstone, J. (2002). Efflorescences and economic growth in world history: Rethinking the rise of the west and the industrial revolution. *Journal of World History, 13*(2), 323–389.

Goldstone, J. (2008). *Why Europe? The rise of the west in world history 1500–1850*. New York: McGraw Hill.

Goldstone, J. (2019). Data and dating the great divergence. In T. Roy & G. Riello (Eds), *Global economic history* (pp. 39–54). London: Bloomsbury Academic.

Goody, J. (2010). *The Eurasian miracle*. Cambridge: Cambridge University Press.

Gregory, J. (2003). *The west and China since 1500*. Basingstoke: Palgrave Macmillan.

Hatcher, J., & Stephenson, J. (Eds.). (2018). *Seven centuries of unreal wages*. Cham: Springer.

Hobson, J. (2004). *The eastern origins of western civilization*. Cambridge: Cambridge University Press.

Howell, M. (2010). *Commerce before capitalism 1300–1600*. Cambridge: Cambridge University Press.

Jones, E. (1987). *The European miracle. Environments, economies and geopolitics in the history of Europe and Asia*. Cambridge: Cambridge University Press.

Kuroda, A. (2013). What was the Silver Tael System? A mistake of China as a Silver 'Standard Country'. In G. Depeyrot (Ed.), *Three conferences on international monetary history*. Moneta: Wetteron.

Kuznets, S. (1966). *Modern economic growth*. New Haven: Yale University Press.

Kuznets, S. (1971). *The economic growth of nations*. Cambridge, MA: Harvard University Press.

Lebow, R. N., Tetlock, P., & Parker, G. (Eds.). (2006). *Unmaking of the west: What if scenarios that rewrote world history*. Ann Arbor: Michigan University Press.

Leonard, J., & Watt, J. (Eds.). (1992). *To achieve security and wealth. The Qing Imperial State and the economy, 1644–1912*. Ithaca: Cornell University Press.

Lieberman, V. (2009). *Strange parallels. South-East Asia in global context. C. 800–1830: Vol. II—Mainland mirrors: Europe, Japan, China, South Asia and the Islands*. Cambridge, MA: Harvard University Press.

Li, B., & Van Zanden, J-L. (2012). Before the great divergence? Comparing the Yangtze Delta at the beginning of the nineteenth century. *Journal of Economic History, 72*, 956–989.

Macfarlane, A. (2014). *The invention of the modern world*. Les Brouzils: Fortnightly Press.

Maddison, A. (2007). *Chinese economic performance in the long run, 960–2030* (2nd ed.). Paris: OECD Publications Service.

Marks, S. (2016). *Global capitalism, from the renaissance to the present*. Cambridge: Cambridge University Press.

Naquin, S., & Rawski, E. (1987). *Chinese society in the eighteenth century*. New Haven: Yale University Press.

Parthasarathi, P. (2010). *Why Europe grew rich and Asia did not: Global economic divergence, 1600–1850*. Cambridge: Cambridge University Press.

Perkins, D. (1969). *Agricultural development in China 1868–1968*. Edinburgh: Aldine Publishing Company.

Perrson, K. (2010). *An economic history of Europe*. Cambridge: Cambridge University Press.

Pomeranz, K. (2000). *The great divergence: China, Europe and the making of the modern world economy*. Princeton: Princeton University Press.

Rawski, T., & Li, L. (Eds.). (1992). *Chinese history in economic perspective*. Oxford: Oxford University Press.

Ringmar, E. (2007). *Why Europe was first? Social and economic growth in Europe and East Asia, 1500–1850*. New York: Anthem Press.

Rowe, W. (2009). *China's last empire: The great Qing*. London: Belknap Press of Harvard University Press.

Roy, T., & Riello, G. (Eds.). (2019). *Global economic history*. London: Bloomsbury Academic.

Shi, Z. (2018). *Agricultural development in Qing China: A quantitative study, 1661–1911*. Leiden: Brill.

So, B. L. (Ed.). (2013). *The economy of the lower Yangzi Delta in late imperial China*. London: Routledge.

Stiglitz, J. E., Anand, S., & Segal, P. (Eds.) (2010). *Debates on the Measurement of Global Poverty*. Oxford: Oxford University Press.

Von Glahn, R. (2016). *The economic history of China from antiquity to the nineteenth century*. Cambridge: Cambridge University Press.

Vanhaute, E. (Ed.) (2015). Escaping the great divergence. *The Low Countries Journal of Social and Economic History, 12*(2), 3–16.

Van Zanden, J.-L., & Ma, D. (2017). What makes Maddison right? Chinese historic economic data. *World Economics, 18*, 2.

Vries, P. (2015). *State economy and the great divergence: Great Britain and China 1680s–1850s*. London: Bloomsbury.

Wood, E. (2002). *The origins of capitalism—A longer view*. New York: Verso.

CHAPTER 3

# Environments and Natural Resources

**Abstract** Two theses are elaborated in this chapter. They will be analysed in greater detail in Chapters 4, 5 and 6. Imperial China's long-established position as the world's most successful organic economy was based upon the advantages of ecological diversity. Divergence relative to Europe began to occur and persist largely because these advantages diminished over time. Environmental historians (Elvin, Marks, Pomeranz and others) correctly insist that foundational geographical facts and China's long history of extensive development to its production possibility boundaries should continue to be accorded greater weight and significance than Eurocentred criticisms of the Empire's state, culture and institutions have recognized. Environmental, political and geopolitical parameters established conditions within which cycles of demographic recovery and economic growth operated to sustain high standards of living for the Empire's population until latent Malthusian forces, combined with environmental degradation and a major political conjuncture disturbed a benign physiocratic equilibrium. Meanwhile seaborne trade with the Baltic and Russia provided the backward but converging economies of Western Europe with supplies of grain, fish, timber, iron, pitch, tar, flax, hemp and other organic inputs needed for early transitions to industrial market economies. Europe also possessed and before China began to exploit the fuel and energy embodied in massive reserves of cheap transportable coal. Finally, Europeans discovered and gradually derived truly

© The Author(s), under exclusive license to Springer Nature      31
Switzerland AG 2020
P. K. O'Brien, *The Economies of Imperial China
and Western Europe*, Palgrave Studies in Economic
History, https://doi.org/10.1007/978-3-030-54614-4_3

32  P. K. O'BRIEN

enormous economic benefits from the fertile land, timber, fuel, arboreal products, minerals and bullion available for exploitation in the Americas. The "bounty" was, moreover, realized by rising flows of migrants to the new world of Europe's young healthy skilled but underemployed adults and more significantly, by the forcible transportation of millions of African slaves to the Americas to labour on plantations and in mines located in inhospitable climates for white emigrants. These two theses support the view that the late Ming and Qing China lacked access to anything comparable to the volume of resources that (fortuitously) became available to early modern Western Europe. The Manchu regime took over an empire at a time in its history when the economy became confronted by an intensification of demographic pressures as well as new and potentially more serious challenges to internal order and external security.

**Keywords** Land: Arable and pastoral · Cultivated and cropped · Natural resources · Environmental depletion and degradation · Organic/physiocratic economy · Irrigation · Malthusian/Ricardian pressures · Internal order · External security

Given that there is very little high ground to be gained by continuing to engage in battles over data, the Divergence Debate has now sensibly moved on (Deng and O'Brien 2017), First and foremost to engage with theses prioritized by environmental historians who continue to maintain that early modern Europe began to benefit from underexploited endowments of fossil fuels as well as increasing access to natural resources overseas at a time when China's long-established position as the world's most successful organic economy (based largely upon the advantages of ecological diversity) began to diminish. They insist that these foundational geographical facts should be accorded greater weight and significance than recent and traditional Eurocentred criticisms of the empire's state, culture and institutions have recognized (Brenner and Isett 2002).

Indeed as the debate currently stands the arguments and counterarguments at its core can be distinguished between historians who interpret the rise of the west and the retardation of China, largely in environmental terms from economists and other social scientists predisposed to insist upon mobilizing ambiguous statistics that supposedly refer to the unmeasurable economic, political, institutional and cultural deficiencies of late Ming and, particularly of Qing China (Dixin and Chengming 2000). Furthermore, prominent and difficult to countervail arguments

# 3 ENVIRONMENTS AND NATURAL RESOURCES    33

elaborated by Pomeranz, Perdue, Marks and other sinologists, continue to undermine arguments that evade or minimize the significance of underexploited natural resources for Europe's pre-industrial catch up or convergence stage in comparisons with China (Perdue 1982; Pomeranz 2000; Marks 2012). Yes, seaborne trade with the Baltic and Russia provided the backward but converging economies of Western Europe with elastic supplies of grain, fish, timber, iron, pitch, tar, hemp, flax and other organic inputs needed for their early transitions to industrial urban market economies (Grigg 1980; Warde et al. 2013).

Secondly, and yes again, it was the case that Europe possessed and before China began to intensively exploit the fuel and energy embodied in massive reserves of cheap transportable coal. That reserve of energy allowed European economies to convert millions of hectares of forests into pastoral and arable farmland and thereby alleviated potential Malthusian pressures arising from accelerated rates of population growth and urbanization (Malamina 2009; Campbell and Overton 2010; Barbier 2011). Finally, Europeans discovered and gradually derived truly enormous economic benefits from the cultivable land, timber, fuel, aboreal products, minerals and bullion available for exploitation in the Americas (Jones 1987). That bounty was, however, realized and augmented many times over by the release and migration to a new world of abundant natural resources by a surplus of Europe's young, underemployed male adults and perhaps, more significantly, by the forcible, but profitable, transportation of millions of African slaves across the Atlantic on European ships to labour on plantations and in mines located in climates and conditions that were inhospitable for white emigrants in tropical regions of the Americas? (Hobson 2004; Broadberry and O'Rourke 2010).

*Prima facie* this familiar history of intra-European and trans-Atlantic trade continues to lend support to the view that Ming and Qing China simply lacked access to anything approximating to the range and volume of resources that became fortuitously available to early modern Western Europe at a conjuncture in its history when the empire was confronted by an intensification of demographic pressures, environmental degradation as well as new potential challenges to internal order and external security that the empire had not experienced since the expulsion of the Mongols by a Han Chinese dynasty (the Ming) in 1368 (Fairbank 1978). Although these malign environmental and political threats to the empire's productivity and standards of living could be contained it has long been and continues to be normal for populations of economies to deplete and depreciate the natural resources located within their frontiers. The rates at which that has occurred historically has depended upon: the overall size and growth of populations; prospects for extending (and defending) political frontiers within which known resources (particularly cultivable land) could be exploited in safety; the accumulation over time of knowledge and capital to augment and upgrade the useful and consumable outputs produced per unit of cultivable land; volumes of water, frost free days and other natural resources available to sustain populations of all organic economies (Pomeranz 1993; Sierferle and Breuninger 2003; Acemoglu and Robinson 2012; Deng 2015).

Unfortunately there is no way of quantifying the well-informed views of historical geographers and, latterly, modern environmental historians (with global perspectives) that for centuries the populations of imperial China probably retained access to a superior and more varied endowment of natural resources (including fecund land, minerals, internal waterways, fertile deltas and diverse ecological zones) that favoured the cultivation of greater volumes and ranges of food crops and raw materials, compared to the resources and ecological conditions confronting most populations and societies of Western Europe (Gernet 1982; Malamina 2009; Van Zanden 2009; Marks 2012).

Abbreviating millennia of China's variegated agrarian history into paragraphs simplifies this traditional perception of divergence between Europe and China. Neverthless, it allows for an analysis of contrasts that accord primacy to a conjuncture in the agrarian history of the empire when the bases for the continuation of prior and successful developments were beginning to be seriously and irreversibly eroded by intensifying pressures from population growth linked to environmental degradation and political disorder (Elvin 1996, 2004).

Before the advent of the Ming dynasty and over millennia of time, the empire's arable and pastoral farmland had expanded enormously to adopt an increasing variety of crops and animals, watered to some extent by rain but largely irrigated by water drawn from China's rivers, streams and lakes and by capital formation in an extensive network of man-made canals, waterways, wells and paddy fields (Bray 1986; Deng 1993; Goody 2010).

The mix of foodstuffs and raw materials produced by Chinese farmers diversified from rice, wheat and other staple grains to include: tea, sugar, fruits, spices, herbs and raw materials such as timber, ramie, hemp, cotton and famously, silk (Mazumdar 1998). Regional and local specializations emerged to take advantage of the rich diversity of China's soils, climates, elevations and waterways (Huang 1990). Possibilities for trade were extended and maintained by widening, deepening and diverting the course of rivers, constructing canals and maintaining roads in order to integrate provinces, towns and villages into markets for increasing levels of intra-imperial commerce—supplemented by small volumes of overseas trade (Deng 1999),

Agrarian knowledge based upon observation and learning by farming improved over time. Best practice techniques and ecologically viable crops diffused across the regions of an empire utilizing a common language as well as an early development of printed forms of communication (Huang 1985; Deng 1993). For an era when transportation overland remained costly, China's markets became well connected by waterways for long and short distance commerce. While useful local knowledge seems, moreover, to have been widely and easily diffused (Elvin 1973; Gates 1996).

For centuries the empire may well have occupied a pole position as the world's leading organic economy with relatively high levels of inter-regional trade and efflorescences in the innovations required to exploit the potential embodied in a rich portfolio of natural resources (Adshead 1995; Barbier 2011).

Furthermore and for most of the Ming period 1368–1644 the Malthusian prospect that diminishing returns from intensified depletion and depreciation of the empire's natural endowments might predictably accompany accelerated rates of population growth and become serious and widespread enough to produce conditions leading to a static or possibly declining standard of living had for several reasons been held in check (Twitchett and Mote 1988; Rawski and Li 1992; Lee and Wang 1999; *European Review of Economic History Symposium* 2008).

Firstly, because adverse fluctuations in climate together with episodic warfare against nomads maintained mortality rates at high levels until the second half of the seventeenth century. Secondly, potentially landless families continued to enjoy access to land, water and other resources beyond and above the traditional extensive margins for the cultivation of land. Thirdly, the diffusion of knowledge supported by intra-imperial trade introduced new crops and techniques and promoted the location of agrarian production in ecologically less favourable locations (Brook 1998; Brandt and Rawski 2008). Above all, China's agriculture had concentrated on a staple grain, rice which embodied far higher calorific yields per unit of cropped land than wheat and other staple grains which provided subsistence for Europeans (Kander 2013; Bray et al. 2015; Shi 2018).

These environmental features of the empire rested upon an economy that was overwhelmingly agrarian in nature and operated within a framework of support and rules for internal order and external security that were provided more or less effectively by a Han Chinese regime with limited capacity or pretensions to either intervene in the day-to-day operations of an agrarian economy or to fund the infrastructural capital required for future agrarian and industrial progress (Scott 2008). For example, and apart from occasional ventures of aggression to extend the territory under its rule, the Ming state concentrated the limited revenues it managed to obtain from taxation upon relieving the empire's population from nature's afflictions, such as floods, fluctuations in harvests and to subsidize the resettlement of surplus populations in regions of the empire with uncultivated virgin land (Will 1990; Wong 1997). To represent rather than effectively enforce imperial rule, Chinese emperors recruited on merit (displayed in an imperial examination system,) a small army of officials educated in Confucian moral philosophy, to supervise the dispensation of justice in local disputes and to oversee compliance with demands for taxation from a remote central government (Elman, 2000). By far the largest proportion of revenues under control of the central state was allocated, however, for the construction of fortifications (the Great Wall) and to support troops stationed along China's western and northern frontiers to protect the territory, property and population of the empire against omnipresent threats of predatory raids from nomadic warrior tribes or far more serious invasions of the kind that had led to the conquest and takeover of the Song empire by Mongol warriors between 1279 and 1368 (Brook 2010; Vries 2015).

That destructive conquest which seriously reduced the size of the Han population and economy left an enduring influence upon the defensive and geopolitical policies pursued by the Ming dynasty. The presence of militarily powerful tribes of mounted warriors along its frontiers virtually contained the empire's area of cultivable land that could be settled and farmed in safety. Nevertheless, and within a containable environmental and geopolitical limit, China's farmers developed the economy along traditional lines by exploiting the empire's land, waterways and diverse ecologies for the production of a felicitous mix of crops for subsistence along with trade and specialization that supported a growing population and a small fiscal base. For some 270 years that strategy generated sufficient revenues for external security, internal order and taxation levied by a Han Chinese regime upon a population and an agrarian economy recovering from the infamous Mongol conquest which was perhaps the most severe external shock in its long history as an empire (Deng 1999; Brook 2005).

These environmental and geopolitical parameters together with the extraordinary power that Confucian moral and political philosophy exercised over the behaviour of Chinese officialdom and a society of patriarchal families established conditions within which trends and cycles for demographic recovery and economic growth with social welfare evolved under dynastic Ming rule. Until that is latent Malthusian forces, combined with environmental degradation and a major political and geopolitical conjuncture disturbed an equilibrium that had provided peace, stability and a relatively high standard of living for millions of Chinese families who had lived and laboured within the Ming empire (Hayami and Tsubouchi 1989; Huang 1990; Brook 2005).

Although its relative "significance" continues to be even more difficult to measure than GDP, or real wages, Ken Pomeranz, Robert Marks and the California School have placed the environmental constraints that confronted the Chinese empire as well as the economies of Western Europe over early modern times at the centre of analytical narratives for the Great Divergence. As sinologists) but with the linguistic skills, expertise and scholarly credentials required to comprehend and compare the economic histories of Europe as well as China), they have read enough historical evidence to argue that by, but not before, some contestable period in the eighteenth century the hitherto retarded organic economies of Western Europe had reached a plateau of possibilities to support a rise in the productivity of labour employed in agriculture, industry and services sufficient to promote transitions to urban industrial market economies (Marks 1998; Pomeranz 2000; Lieberman 2009).

In their view that prospect, potential and stimulus evolved in sequence into modern industrial development in Europe basically because the supplies of food, inorganic energy and raw materials as well as the overseas markets, required to support the kind of industrialization, urbanization and trade that marked the rise of the west became (for what they consider to be largely fortuitous reasons) more achievable than anything available to the advanced organic economy of Ming China. The implication is that the resources required to sustain the structural changes for the employment and relocation of European workforces could not have been mobilized in the same way or rate by the already advanced organic and imperial economy of China (Wong 1997; Goldstone 2008). By late Ming times, when the population had more or less recovered from a "fortunately" rather brief period of Mongol conquest and rule, Chinese standards of living became slowly but increasingly constrained by inelastic supplies of land and natural resources as well as the capacities to manage to control over the empire's waterways for irrigation and transportation. Penalties from China's early start were intensifying (Deng 1993; Elvin and Liu 1998).

Nevertheless, in their controversial and heuristic endeavours to undermine Eurocentric views of the late imperial economy the California School seem less inclined than a previous generation of historians of China to recognize that even before the conquest and takeover of the empire by Manchu warriors from the Steppes signs had appeared that the capacities of fecund lowlands and its controllable waterways to support ever-increasing numbers of families at constant ratios of land to labour, together with effectively controlled flows of water for the production and transportation of food and raw materials was not and could not be sustained. By the time of the Manchu takeover the empire's economy and fiscal base had already entered into what Mark Elvin so memorably described as a "high level equilibrium trap" (Elvin 1973).

His seminal analysis of 1973 has been neither disputed, elaborated upon nor taken forward by scholars of the California School. Their preoccupations have been provocatively concentrated on exposing fortuitous benefits that Western Europe supposedly derived from underexploited territories to the east of that sub-continent, and from the exploitation of natural resources in the Americas, combined with the enslavement of human resources from Africa. In short, their explicable predisposition has been to downplay the significance of the endogenous components for the Great Divergence that continued however to evolve along an avoidable trajectory for economic growth leading to diminishing returns (Pomeranz 2000; Xue 2007).

In summary, the revisionist view is that China recovered from the destruction associated with the Manchu conquest and takeover the empire (1636–83) and under a new dynasty the empire adapted more or less effectively to Malthusian pressures and accelerated population growth (Li 1998). In reacting to Eurocentric ignorance of Chinese history and pursuing a benign view of the Qing regime, Ken Pomeranz together with Bozhong Li and other agrarian historians have concentrated attention upon the more commercialized and advanced agricultural regions of China—such as Jiangnan—where industrious peasantries and their families intensified the input of an enlarged amount of labour time at their disposal along several traditional lines (Li and Van Zanden 2012). First and foremost, farmers multiplied the number of crops harvested over the seasons from a given area of land. They reclaimed land from swamps and from areas liable to flooding, extended margins for cultivations up hillsides and into wet lowlands liable to flooding. They imported more night soil from towns and soya bean cake from Manchuria to fertilize their fields. They introduced new world crops such as peanuts, tobacco, potatoes and maize into their rotations. Wherever opportunities existed they specialized on cash crops for which their farmland possessed ecological advantages (Li 1998; So 2013). Finally, rural China's households allocated a rising share of the underemployed labour time of women, children and poor kin to the domestic production of ramie and silk and increasingly to cotton textiles (Rawski and Li 1992).

Few Eurocentric suggestions have appeared in the divergence debate to claim that the farmers of late imperial China failed to apply traditional, relevant and proven techniques for the cultivation of crops or the rearing of animals that could conceivably have sustained even higher yields per hectare on the smaller plots of farmland that they cultivated ever more intensively even in these fecund provinces of China (Hung 2008). Furthermore (and this point has been endorsed by Pomeranz) no argument has been elaborated or documented to support a case that the reallocation of the labour time available to underemployed farm families to the domestic production and sales of fibres, yarns, threads and cloth manufactured from cotton, ramie and silk was sufficient to compensate for an, alas, unmeasurable overall decline in the land/labour ratios. On the contrary, a calibrated shift in the net barter terms of trade between the relative prices of staple grains and cotton textiles suggests that the opposite may have occurred as relatively poor farm families from ecologically disadvantaged regions located in the interior of the empire entered the intra-imperial market for the sale of cheap textiles and depressed a potential for the continuation and increase in overall gains from trade and specialization (Chao 1977; Lebow et al. 2006).

Finally, neither Pomeranz nor the majority of scholars who support the controversial theses that he elaborated so eloquently and persuasively in his seminal book now claim that even the advanced and most industrialized regions of the late Ming economy had evolved to a stage of development from where the structural and technological changes associated with transitions to urban industrialized market economies seemed in prospect or retrospect to have been probable, or as Pomeranz recently wrote in *Historically Speaking* "any time soon" (*Historically Speaking*, September 2011).

On the contrary, and regardless of trajectories that various national economies of Europe may or may not have been on around the time of the protracted geopolitical transition from Ming to Qing dynastic rule, recent scholarship in the new environmental history of China (inspired by Mark Elvin) has exposed an agriculture that, to quote Edward Vermeer, had "entered into a new phase of definitive and irreversible change" (Elvin and Liu 1998). Entry to that potentially more malign Malthusian and commonplace stage in the punctuated evolution of organic economies undergoing Smithian growth had appeared with regionally confined upswings in population growth together with increased inter-regional migration by late Ming times. Thereafter, the alas unmeasurable internal migration of Chinese families onto the empire's less fecund uplands and/or to lands vulnerable to floods or droughts became an unmistakable and persistent problem once the new Qing dynasty had conquered and restored peace and a protracted worldwide spell of unfavourable temperatures and precipitation came to a close (Millward 1998; So 2013). These malign conditions had fortuitously maintained mortality at high rates for several decades of the seventeenth century. By the closing decades of that century major and increasingly serious forces afflicting the very foundations of China's agrarian economy proceeded in ways that both facilitated, but at the same time, gradually denuded the capacities of the empire's cultivable area to cope with continuous increases in population. While fiscal constraints and a slow rate of structural change compared to industrializing Europe hardly alleviated the empire's core problem (Will 1990; Li 2007; Elvin 2010).

The multiple ways in which the Chinese dealt with this intensified Malthusian "phase of irreversible change" has been surveyed in an impressive bibliography of history published in recent years by its agrarian and demographic historians. Their concerns have been concerned to elaborate on how population pressures led inexorably by way of environmental degradation to a decline from a modal standard of living that had for millennia sustained the empire's population at a level some way above the modern scientifically prescribed intake of 2300 kilocalories per capita per day required for food security (Huang 1985, 1990; Perkins 1969; So 2013).

However, and as Malthus and Ricardo predicted, and the Elvin School has documented environmental depletion and degradation flowed from the intensification of multiple cropping, from eroding the thinner soils of hills, from terracing the landscape, from exploiting large areas of China's forests for fuel and timber and above all, from reclaiming woodland for arable farming. Reclamation involved the felling of trees growing on uplands along extensive margins for cultivation which eroded surrounding soils and destroyed natural buffers against flows of soil, silt and stones carried by rainwater into the rivers and streams connected to manmade channels of the empire's extensive systems for irrigation and waterborne transport. The defence, maintenance and repair of that long-established network of natural and constructed waterways against the ravages of uncontrolled flows of water from uplands to the alluvial and fertile lowlands had long been an outstanding achievement of Chinese agriculture. By the late Ming dynasty increased demands for fuel and timber as well as cultivable land shifted the share of an increased flow of internal migration and settlement of landless families away from the deltas, plains and fertile lowlands towards the uplands and also into more vulnerable and hostile areas of the empire for cultivation (Elvin and Liu 1998; Elvin 2004; Marks 2012).

In the absence of significant technological innovations the costs of the investment, labour, raw materials and the complexities of the organization and coordination required to maintain agricultural output per capita at traditional levels must surely have emerged as China's persistent and ever-intensifying problem. The Manchu's took over an agrarian empire at a time in its long history when the depletion of natural resources and diminishing returns to traditional ways of utilizing coordinating and controlling water had set in (Perdue 1982; Tvedt 2010). Historical understanding has now overtaken the Eurocentred and heuristic debate on the Great Divergence. That conjuncture can continue, however, to be represented as a Malthusian period in the long history of an advanced organic economy which displayed limited prospects or potential for structural change along European lines. The Qing empire coped with these problems, but in a traditional Chinese way with a state and under a new regime that clearly was not up to the task of precluding retardation compared to Western Europe (Rowe 2009; Acemoglu and Robinson 2012).

# REFERENCES

Acemoglu, D., & Robinson, J. (2012). *Why nations fail: The origins of power, prosperity and poverty*. London: Crown Publishing.

Adshead, S. (1995). *China in world history*. London: Palgrave Macmillan.

Barbier, E. (2011). *Scarcity and frontiers: How economies have developed through natural resource exploitation*. Cambridge: Cambridge University Press.

Brandt, L., & Rawski, T. (Eds.). (2008). *China's great transformation*. Cambridge: Cambridge University Press.

Bray, F., Coclanis, P. A., & Fields-Black, E. L. (2015). *Rice, global networks and new histories*. Cambridge: Cambridge University Press.

Bray, F. (1986). *The rice economies: Technology and development in Asian societies*. London: University of California Press.

Brenner, R., & Isett, C. (2002). England's divergence from China's Yangtze Delta: Property relations, microeconomics and patterns of development. *Journal of Asian Studies, 61*, 609–662.

Broadberry, S., & O'Rourke, K. (2010). *The Cambridge economic history of modern Europe. Vol. 1. 1700–1800*. Cambridge: Cambridge University Press.

Brook, T. (1998). *The confusions of pleasure, commerce and culture in Ming China*. Berkeley: California University Press.

Brook, T. (2005). *The Chinese state in Ming society*. London: Routledge.

Brook, T. (2010). *The troubled empire. China in the Yuan and Ming dynasties*. Cambridge, MA: Harvard University Press.

Campbell, B., & Overton, M. (2010). *Agricultural revolution in England: The transformation of the agricultural economy*. Cambridge: Cambridge University Press.

Chao, G. (1977). *The development of cotton textile production in China*. Cambridge, MA: Harvard University Press.

Deng, G. (1993). *Development versus stagnation: Technological continuity and agricultural progress in pre-modern China*. Westport: Greenwood Press.

Deng, G. (1999). *The pre-modern Chinese economy: Structural equilibrium and capitalist sterility*. London: Routledge.

Deng, K. (2015). *Mapping China's growth and development in the long run 221BC to 2020*. Singapore: World Scientific Publishing.

Deng, K., & O'Brien, P. (2017). How far back in time might macro- economic facts travel? The debate on the great divergence: Imperial China and the West. *World Economics, 18*, 2.

Dixin, X., & Chengming, W. (Eds.). (2000). *Chinese capitalism 1522–1840*. London: Palgrave Macmillan.

Elman, B. (2000). *A cultural history of civil examinations in late imperial China*. Berkeley: University of California Press.

Elvin, M. (1973). *The pattern of the Chinese past: A social and economic interpretation*. Stanford: Stanford University Press.

Elvin, M. (1996). *Another history: Essays on China from a European perspective.* Honolulu: Wild Peony/University of Hawaii.

Elvin, M. (2004). *The retreat of the elephants: An environmental history of China.* New Haven: Yale University Press.

Elvin, M. (2010). The environmental impasse in late imperial China. In B. Womack (Ed.), *China's rise in historical perspective.* Lanham: Rowman & Littlefield.

Elvin, M., & Liu, T.-J. (Eds.). (1998). *Sediments of time: Environment and society in Chinese history.* Cambridge: Cambridge University Press.

*European Review of Economic History Symposium.* (2008).

Fairbank, J. (Ed.). (1978). *The Cambridge history of China 1800–1911 Vol. 10 The Late Qing.* Cambridge: Cambridge University Press.

Gates, H. (1996). *Chinese motor a thousand years of petty capitalism.* Ithaca: Cornell University Press.

Gernet, J. (1982). *A history of Chinese civilization.* Cambridge: Cambridge University Press.

Goldstone, J. (2008). *Why Europe? The rise of the west in world history 1500–1850.* New York: McGraw Hill.

Goody, J. (2010). *The Eurasian miracle.* Cambridge: Cambridge University Press.

Grigg, D. (1980). *Population growth and agrarian change. A historical perspective.* Cambridge: Cambridge University Press.

Hayami, A., & Tsubouchi, Y. (Eds.). (1989). *Economic and demographic development in rice producing societies: Some aspects of East Asian History 1500–1700.* Leuven: Leuven University Press.

Hobson, J. (2004). *The eastern origins of western civilization.* Cambridge: Cambridge University Press.

Huang, P. (1985). *The peasant economy and social change in North China.* Stanford: Stanford University Press.

Huang, P. (1990). *The peasant family and rural development in the Yangtze Delta 1350–1988.* Stanford: Stanford University Press.

Hung, H-F. (2008). Agricultural revolution and elite reproduction in Qing China. *American Sociological Review, 73,* 569–588.

Jones, E. (1987). *The European miracle. Environments, economies and geopolitics in the history of Europe and Asia.* Cambridge: Cambridge University Press.

Lebow, R. N., Tetlock, P., & Parker, G. (Eds.). (2006). *Unmaking of the west: What if scenarios that rewrote world history.* Ann Arbor: Michigan University Press.

Lee, J., & Wang, F. (1999). *One quarter of humanity: Malthusian mythology and Chinese realities.* Cambridge, MA: Harvard University Press.

Li, B. (1998). *Agricultural development in Jiangnan 1620–1850.* London: Palgrave Macmillan.

44   P. K. O'BRIEN

Li, B., & Van Zanden, J-L. (2012). Before the great divergence? Comparing the Yangtze Delta at the beginning of the nineteenth century. *Journal of Economic History, 72,* 956–989.

Li, L. (2007). *Fighting famine in North China: State, market and environmental decline.* Stanford: Stanford University Press.

Lieberman, V. (2009). *Strange parallels. South-East Asia in global context, c. 800– 1830. Vol. II, Mainland Mirrors: Europe, Japan, China, South Asia and the Islands.* Cambridge, MA: Harvard University Press.

Malamina, P. (2009). *Pre-modern European Economy: One thousand years—10th– 19th centuries.* Leiden: Brill.

Marks, R. (1998). *Tigers, rice, silk and silt: Environment and economy in Late Imperial South China.* Cambridge: Cambridge University Press.

Marks, R. (2012). *China: Its environment and its history.* New York: Rowan & Littlefield.

Mazumdar, S. (1998). *Sugar and society in China: Peasants society and the world market.* London: Harvard University Press.

Millward, J. (1998). *Beyond the pass: Economy, ethnicity in Qing Central Asia 1759–1864.* Stanford: Stanford University Press.

Perdue, P. (1982). Water control in the Dongting lake region during the Ming and Qing periods. *Journal of Asian Studies, 41,* 747–765.

Perkins, D. (1969). *Agricultural development in China 1368–1968.* Edinburgh: Edinburgh University Press.

Pomeranz, K. (1993). *The making of a hinterland: State, society, and economy in inland North China, 1853–1937.* Berkeley: University of California Press.

Pomeranz, K. (2000). *The great divergence: China, Europe and the making of the modern world economy.* Princeton: Princeton University Press.

Rawski, T., & Li, L. (Eds.). (1992). *Chinese history in economic perspective.* Oxford: Oxford University Press.

Rowe, W. (2009). *China's last empire: The great Qing.* London: Belknap Press of Harvard University Press.

Scott, A. (2008). *The evolution of resource property rights.* Oxford: Oxford University Press.

Sierferle, R., & Breuninger, H. (Eds.). (2003). *Agriculture, population and development in China and Europe.* Stuttgart: Breuninger Stiftung GmbH.

Shi, Zhihong. (2018). *Agricultural development in Qing China.* Leiden: Brill.

So, B. (Ed.). (2013). *The economy of the lower Yangtze delta in late imperial China.* London: Routledge.

Tvedt, T. (2010). Why England not China and India? Water systems and the history of the industrial revolution. *Journal of Global History, 5,* 29–50.

Twitchett, D., & Mote, F. (Eds.). (1988). *The Cambridge history of China, Vol. 8 The Ming Dynasty.* Cambridge: Cambridge University Press.

Van Zanden, J-L. (2009). *The long road to the industrial revolution: The European economy in global perspective, 1000–1800*. Leiden: Brill.

Von Glahn, R. (2016). *The economic history of China: From antiquity to the nineteenth century*. Cambridge: Cambridge University Press.

Vries, P. (2015). *State economy and the great divergence: Great Britain and China 1680s–1850s*. London: Bloomsbury.

Warde, P., Kander, A., & Malanima, P. (2013). *Power to the people: Energy in Europe over the last five centuries*. Princeton: Princeton University Press.

Will, P-E. (1990). State intervention in the administration of a hydraulic infrastructure: The example of Hubei Province in late imperial times. In *Bureaucracy and famine in eighteenth century China*. Stanford: Stanford University Press.

Wong, R. B. (1997). *China transformed: Historical change and the limits of European experience*. Ithaca: Cornell University Press.

Xue, Y (2007). A fertilizer revolution A critical response to Pomeranz's theory of geographical luck. Modern China, 33.

Zelin, M., Ocko, J. K., & Gardella, R. (Eds.). (2004). *Contract and property in early modern China*. Stanford: Stanford University Press.

CHAPTER 4

# The Ming and Qing Imperial States and Their Agrarian Economies

**Abstract** No participant in the Divergence Debate has argued that the problems of an agrarian empire that had successfully exploited its rich natural resources to reach a production possibility frontier of diminishing returns could have been anything but complex and costly to solve. The issue specified in this chapter is what options were realistically available to the state to alleviate problems becoming increasingly acute from the demise of the Ming in the seventeenth century onwards? Could those options have conceivably included industrialization and structural change along western lines? From a Eurocentred perspective this option may be plausibly dismissed as too anachronistic to contemplate. Thus the retardation of China may, therefore, continue to be represented as endogenous. Furthermore and without some conceivable reforms to the empire's financial and monetary systems, the range of strategies available to the state for defence against western aggression, the maintenance of internal order and positive interventions to raise investment in the empire's depreciating infrastructure for agrarian development at both extensive and intensive margins for cultivation remained severely circumscribed. In short, the core of any historical narrative for divergence includes penalties attached to an early start and a long term failure of the Ming and Qing regimes to create a state with the fiscal resources and executive systems for the governance of an empire with a successful organic and physiocratic economy.

© The Author(s), under exclusive license to Springer Nature
Switzerland AG 2020
P. K. O'Brien, *The Economies of Imperial China
and Western Europe*, Palgrave Studies in Economic
History, https://doi.org/10.1007/978-3-030-54614-4_4

47

48    P. K. O'BRIEN

**Keywords** Fiscal capacity · State formation · Bureaucracy · Public goods · Internal order · External security · Imperial expansion · International and external migration · Common resources · Reciprocal but anachronistic comparisons

Economic historians recognize that transitions to modern economic growth over centuries of time and are promoted by the establishment and maintenance of interconnected sets of institutions. That evolution was, moreover, sustained or alternatively constrained by the strategic investments and economic policies pursued by states and their nominally subordinated elites. Current "Eurocentred views" are that for albeit explicable historical, geographical, political, geopolitical, economic and cultural reasons China's imperial state failed to establish and maintain institutions that could be represented as fit to deal with the Malthusian challenges faced by the populations and communities of the mid Ming and early Qing empires, 1368–1911 (Peyefitte 1992; Vries 2015). Prima facie under both regimes state investment in the agrarian infrastructure and for the extension and integration of markets for commodities, labour and capital has been plausibly depicted as ultimately inadequate for agrarian development with structural change compared to the mercantilist policies pursued by the British and neighbouring states of Western Europe (Rowe 2009; Vries 2013). Furthermore, the imperial state has also been denigrated for failing to encourage the development and adaptation of the scientific and technical knowledge utilized for the production, transportation and distribution of commodities and services; for warfare, defence and internal order as well as public and personal health. In this sphere, its role has been variously represented as indifferent or potentially obstructive towards the formation and diffusion of such knowledge (Leonard and Watt 1992; Duchesne 2011).

The California School has exposed several lines of this traditional Eurocentric critique as anachronistic and ignorant. The School has portrayed the unfavourable representation of the political economy, pursued by successive Ming and Qing governments as biased and lacking in historical understanding of the contexts and priorities accorded to political stability, local outcomes, social order and human welfare by China's imperial regimes compared to policies pursued for power, profit and hierarchy by Europe's more centralized and mercantilist states (Wong 1997; Waley-Cohen 1999; Pomeranz 2000).

Revisionists have, furthermore, attempted to undermine assertions that the statistical records show that for centuries before 1789 European states (particularly Britain) had sustained more favourable sets of institutions for the promotion of long term economic growth. They are especially critical of the tendency among western historians to conclude that Chinese ways of macro-economic management had long been not merely different but inferior to western ways, or that European methods and techniques for economic governance that could, moreover, have been adapted as necessary guidance for a state that was presiding over an organic economy that after 1800 was descending into decline and crises (*American Historical Review Forum* 2002).

Apart from asserting that there is virtually no statistical evidence for serious economic retardation before the late eighteenth century (that for reasons outlined in Chapter 2 turns out to be improbable but alas unmeasurable), the California School's defence of the Chinese state and the institutions it supported for infrastructural investment, production, distribution, exchange, social welfare and technological innovation remains unconvincing (Brook 2005; Goody 2010). Its views have provoked sceptical responses and stimulated a wave of ongoing historical research and debate into the regulations, rules and institutions surrounding the empire's markets for: commodities, capital, labour as well as the accumulation of knowledge that could mature into technologies and modes of organization for purposes of production and defence (Zurndorfer 2016).

The bibliography of recently published historical research that has engaged with well-specified reciprocal comparisons covering the Chinese and a sample of European states and institutions that they supported has become too extensive and detailed to summarize and very difficult to synthesize. Debate on the Great Divergence has certainly rescued the Chinese state from a Eurocentric tradition of condescension for not being or becoming European. Nevertheless, major critiques of the late imperial state and the local elites and institutions it sustained (or failed to replace or reform) in order to deal more effectively with the problems of depletion and depreciation of the empire's infrastructure for agrarian production and trade (let alone for the facilitation of structural change towards mechanized modern industry) have not been refuted (Brandt and Rawski 2008; Kent 2010; Rosenthal and Wong 2011; Tanimoto and Wong 2019).

Foremost and foundational among the critiques of the Ming and Qing regimes must be their prolonged failure to construct the fiscal, financial and monetary institutions necessary to fund affordable policies to cope with demographic pressures accompanied by rising levels of disorder and (after takeovers of the Philippines, Java and India) the looming threat posed by western imperialism to the external security of the vastly expanded territorial empire under the control of the Qing regime (Leonard and Watt 1992; Dunstan 1996; Elliott 2001; Peterson 2002).

Predictably even the significance of this unquantified but theoretically quantifiable critique has proved difficult to test because comprehensive accounts of total expenditures (or for their proxy total revenues) allocated by a command from the central state for imperial macro-economic and social welfare purposes were not available either to the empire's ruling elites appropriating and allocating taxes and rents at the time, or to modern historians today (Feuerwerker 1973). Official records for a sample of years from 1683 to 1839 for the states' dominant source of income (the land tax) have survived (Wang 1973). But almost all other forms of "proto taxation" appropriated and expropriated for purposes of funding the provision of goods and services by the state—such as corvée labour, profits from the sale of titles, degrees, offices and monopoly rights were rarely recorded in any systematic way. Another and perhaps quantitively significant but unrecorded source of "public" revenue was extorted in the name of the state from its subjects by a tiny bureaucracy of underpaid appointed officials who were compelled to employ and somehow remunerate a much larger workforce of "unofficial" locally recruited clerks, runners and other assistants in order to provide public goods and services in their localities and to assess the population's liabilities for taxation within and across the counties, provinces and prefectures of the vastly expanded Manchu empire (Zelin 1984; Park 1997; Deng 2012).

Histories of early modern state formation in Europe as well as China have exposed the range of coercive expedients that ruling elites resorted to everywhere in order to obtain, maintain and increase revenues and to minimize the unavoidable costs involved in their assessment and collection. Coercive expedients, by undermanned and underfunded fiscal administrations charged to execute this core function in ways and at rates prescribed by central governments rarely became efficacious for maintaining, let alone, extending compliance with demands and needs for the means to fund the provision of public goods and services. On the contrary, institutionalized predation not only operated to reduce the capacities of states to formulate and execute policies for development, but often provoked evasion, resentment, resistance and ultimately serious threats to that core precondition for economic growth—internal order (Gray 2002; O'Brien 2014).

Devolved, inefficient and ramshackle fiscal and financial systems were, however, features of early modern regimes in the Occident as well as the Orient. Thus unless and until data becomes available to compare differences between both the total amounts of revenue appropriated and expropriated from the subjects of European and Chinese states as well as the relative amounts that they allocated towards the provision of public goods, it will remain difficult to actually measure the fiscal and financial capacities of the central imperial state and its subordinate local authorities compared to a sample of altogether smaller European central governments and local authorities (Kent 2010; Karaman and Pamuk 2010).

Fortunately the volume and quality of the secondary literature published on fiscal policy and administration for the empire and for several major European states is certainly superior to most other literatures available for the construction of quantified comparative histories of Europe and China. Thus, and apart from statistical records for the land tax, there is a bibliography of books and articles by experts that deal with the empire's fiscal history at central and local levels (Wong 1997). They cite official data that can be referenced to construct lower bound estimates for total revenues denominated in silver taels that became available to the central state for ad hoc years between 1683 and 1839. Estimates of roughly similar quality are available for several European powers as well as accounts of greater accuracy for the United Kingdom and the Netherlands. Statistics for taxation legally collected and spent locally on public services are not available for China and poorly recorded for most European countries (Deng 2012; Yun-Casalilla and O'Brien 2012).

Unlike the statistical evidence published for GDP per capita, real wages and peasant incomes data in the form of revenues received by central governments seems, however, to be accurate enough to be calibrated in ways that expose the relative capacities of imperial and national states to pursue fundable policies for the provision of public goods. For example, records for total revenues received and/or recorded by states can be divided by their populations, areas of territory and kilometres of frontiers nominally subjected to the authority of the Qing state and compared to the revenues of several occidental states including Britain. These figures can be converted into grams of silver, grain equivalents or days of labour time in order to tabulate plausible conjectures that serve to compare the command that states exercised over the fiscal and financial resources required to implement policies as well as the relative burdens of taxation that they imposed on their subjects. Objections that the statistics for revenues collected and allocated for the provision of public goods and services for the empire by the central Qing state are simply not comprehensive enough to allow for systematic comparisons with the revenues and expenditures undertaken by European states can, moreover, be undermined by multiplying the recorded figures of receipts from the land tax transferred to Beijing by multipliers of 2 or 3 or even 4 in order to offer guestimates for revenues (and by extension the expenditures) undertaken by the state and its subordinated authorities (Liu 2005; Vries 2015).

On the basis of such "counterfactual arithmetic" only a Eurocentred, negative, but statistically plausible view can be taken off the altogether weaker fiscal capacities of the central Qing state to formulate and execute policies to deal with the pressures from population growth, internal disorder, external security and environmental degradation that afflicted the subjects of the empire with increasing intensity after the Manchu dynasty had consolidated its power to rule over a Han Chinese population and expanding territorial empire in 1683 (Karaman and Pamuk 2010; Ma 2014).

A latent Malthusian problem, episodic disorder and perceptions of western threat to the cohesion and security of that empire were, however, already present by the late Ming dynasty (Brook 2010). They became more serious after the Qing takeover even though the reorganization of China's military power by a dynasty of warriors from the steppes of Central Asia solved for all time recurrent invasions by nomadic armies across the frontiers of the empire. That geopolitical threat had persisted despite the high levels of expenditure upon the construction of the Great Wall and the stationing of garrisons of troops along its perimeters (Spence and Mills 1979). Furthermore and not long after the sovereignty of the dynasty had been consolidated Qing armies marched west and in a sequence of campaigns defeated Mongol and other armies along the western and northern frontiers of China. Vast and potentially exploitable territory sparsely populated by Manchus, Mongols, Tibetans and other nomadic peoples and tribes were thereby incorporated into the empire that more than doubled the territory under Qing rule (Perdue 2005; Patterson 2006).

In effect the Manchu conquests of Ming China followed by the expropriation and settlement of territory along its vulnerable frontiers with Central Asia provided the Han Chinese population with the external security against predatory raids and invasions overland which they had sought to contain for centuries (Smith and von Glahn 2003). Manchu imperialism provided potential access to millions of ghost acres of cultivable land, minerals and other natural resources, together with outlets for the surplus of population of the long-settled and over-populated lowlands and river deltas of ancient China. Furthermore, the "peace dividend" that flowed from reductions in expenditures upon fortifications and garrisons along its borders with Central Asia became available as revenues that could have been reallocated to modernize the empire's depreciated infrastructure for production and trade (Struve 2004; Andrade 2016).

Historians of Qing China have accorded proper recognition to the expenditures maintained and even increased on relief from periodic natural disasters from floods, droughts and poor harvests. Subsidies towards the purchase and reclamation of land and resettlement also continued to be extended to landless people. Prudentially perhaps China's "alien" rulers did not neglect to maintain and fund traditional policies for the alleviation of natural disasters or the amelioration of conditions afflicting the empire's rising proportion of poor and landless labourers (Feuerwerker 1992; Wong 1997; Deng 2012).

Nevertheless and apart from these "Confucian" welfare policies (which absorbed relatively small shares of the revenues collected for central and local government) the critique that the imperial regime neither took over nor established fiscal capacities to cope with the demographic pressures arising from an upswing in the rate of population growth seems, in retrospect, difficult to evade.

That underdeveloped capacity remained essentially fiscal because (and in contrast to Europe) neither the Qing nor previous regimes responsible for the management of the empire established the mechanisms and institutions for regularized and systematic recourse and access to credits to facilitate their day-to-day requirements for liquidity, let alone financial institutions to facilitate the raising of long or medium term loans to fund investments in fixed capital formation. Until very late in the nineteenth-century Chinese policy and governance was funded without recourse to the accumulation of sovereign debt. When they occurred sporadic fiscal deficits were solved by coercive demands imposed upon merchants for "contributions" to fund urgent and unavoidable needs for expenditures by the state (Feuerwerker 1992).

Apart from such episodic lapses into predation and confronted by clear evidence for intensified population pressure, the laissez faire strategy pursued by the imperial state can continue to be represented as a major and deeply conservative force in narratives designed to explain divergence in the performance of the Chinese and Western European economies over the long run (Kaske 2017). Regardless of when that divergence became manifest and for whatever fortuitous or commendable reasons, the economic and geopolitical rise of the West occurred, the institutions in place and the strategies pursued for the economic management of an imperial infrastructure for production can only be held responsible for possibly the largest and most significant share of the Qing empire's inadequate if regionally disparate economic performance between 1683 and 1911 (For a more favourable interpretation of the Qing state's economic policies read Wong 1997; Pomeranz 2000; Deng 2012).

Yet, until after the defeat of the most costly and destructive internal rebellion in Chinese history (1850–64), the Qing state did virtually nothing to extend its fiscal base beyond the dominant and traditional tax on agricultural land (supplemented by a levy on the consumption of salt) in order to widen the range of taxes either upon intra-imperial and foreign commerce or on industrial production. Furthermore, the bases and rules for the assessment, collection and transfer of the regime's dominant source of revenue into the coffers of the central state or into the hands of subordinated local authorities, continued for centuries to be neither formulated nor organized in ways that fiscal historians could conceivably recognize as equitable, productive or likely to sustain acceptable degrees of compliance. For example, neither the Ming nor Qing regimes: conducted anything better than a single poorly executed survey to record the empire's area of taxable farmland. They neglected to standardize the "mu"—a local but variable area of cultivable land of disparate fecundities into an imperial unit that could serve as a proxy measure for a reformed base for fiscal extraction (Perkins 1969; Deng and O'Brien 2015). Both landowners and farmers could, moreover, avoid their responsibilities to pay for the needs and priorities of the state. The latter could raise and retain a higher share of output per mu of taxed land by multiple cropping and increased applications of organic fertilizers. While the former could misuse the powers devolved by the state onto local gentry by colluding with a tiny cadre of resident officials responsible for the assessment, collection and allocation of revenues on behalf of an emperor, ruling from far away in Beijing, but mandated from heaven to provide external security, internal stability and relief from natural disasters, for a vast and heterogeneous empire (Chang 1955; Zelin 1984; Waley-Cohen 2006; Rowe 2009).

Furthermore, and under both regimes, liabilities for the land tax continued to be imposed in yet another official but non-standardized unit of monetary account, namely the silver tael. The purchasing power of China's "quasi official" coin over kilocalories of nutrients and labour time as well as local copper currencies in mass circulation varied across space and through time in ways and degrees that added to the uncertainties of the purchasing power embodied in the currency (Kuroda 2013). After 1800 when the bimetallic ratio moved in favour of silver it also augmented burdens on taxpayers (Hirzel and Kim 2008; Horesh 2012).

Fiscal historians who "follow the money" and have concluded that China's tax system concentrated upon a single tax was not designed to promote compliance or assessed effectively enough to reduce the costs of collection, evasion and thereby leave the central Chinese state and local organs of government with sufficient revenues to allocate for the support the empire's increasing requirements for public goods (Deng 2012). Constructive reforms to the fiscal system were mooted after defeat in the First Opium War (1839–42) but hardly occurred before the Taiping rebellion (1850–64) had exposed the failures of the empire's dangerously undermanned and underfunded army to deal with a protracted, massively destructive and almost successful challenge to the sovereignty of the state. Before these disastrous and costly shocks, the Manchu elite (operating as alien rulers of a far flung empire) proceeded with political prudence and Confucian circumspection to govern their empire within the constraints of the fiscal and financial system and ideology that they had inherited from the Ming (Feuerwerker 1995; Deng 2012; He 2013).

As the Jiaqing emperor's edict of 1815 proclaimed "our dynasty does not increase the land tax for all eternity. We collect the regular land tax within the limits of established precedent and grant tax remissions and referrals during droughts and floods. This is because by reducing the state to the benefit of the people, their delight will know no limits. Safeguarding the property of the multitude is the foundation of preserving the dynasty" (Pines 2012; Kaske 2017).

For decades his dynasty had indeed neglected to increase capacities to tax or perhaps borrow sufficient revenues to provide the empire with the military and naval power needed to meet potential and predictable challenges to its external security and internal order, let alone cope with the intensifying problems of advanced agrarian economy undergoing demographic pressures and environmental degradation (Leonard 1968; Dunstan 1996; Waley-Cohen 2006).

No historian of China could pretend that the problems of an agrarian empire, dependent on rising levels of expenditure upon its irrigation systems and which had exploited its natural resources to reach a production possibility frontier of diminishing returns could be anything but costly and complex to solve (Chao 1986; Crossley et al. 2006). Thus, the issue that remains for the Divergence Debate to explore is, what options might be realistically represented as available to the state? Could they possibly have appealed to the Qing regime as policies designed to emulate the strategies pursued by western states that were not at the time perceived to have been path-dependent and simply not transferable to an empire at the other end of Eurasia? Or was the problem of divergence more realistically defined in historical terms as one of endogenous internal Chinese decline which, in retrospect, cannot be excused as basically unavoidable? For historians of China some counterfactuals may well seem worthy of consideration, while others, such as the emulation of a British, Dutch or even French model for economic growth based upon structural change, industrialization and urbanization have been convincingly dismissed as heuristic to contemplate but anachronistic? (Rowe 2009) Few will, however, be prepared to reject the inferences (elaborated above) that without some conceivable programme of gradual reforms to the fiscal, financial and monetary institutions of the empire, the range of options open to the Qing regime for purposeful and positive interventions in the economy seems in retrospect to have been severely circumscribed by failures to engage in fiscal, financial and institutional transformation (Horesh 2014; Vries 2013, 2015).

Lacking the means to command and mobilize resources to reclaim cultivable land at the extensive margins of a vastly enlarged empire and to regulate flows of water onto areas of an increasingly less fecund cultivated area, the Qing state invested very little. It virtually abandoned controls that had operated reasonably well until late Ming times to contain the degradation of irrigated farmland and the deterioration of waterways for transportation and trade.

For millennia the development of Chinese agriculture had been accompanied by the migration of surplus and underemployed people onto farmlands favoured by fertile soils, benign climates, access to tractable waterways and a modicum of state protection against risks from natural disasters and predatory nomads. As the population increased prospects for internal migration, reclamation and settlement on land close to waterways of comparable fecundity and productivity diminished within the extensive margin of fertile lowland areas already under cultivation. While the qualities, locations and accessibilities of the vast territories, rivers, streams and other natural resources that were incorporated into the empire by Manchu-led conquests lacked clear economic potential and attractions for migrants from more productive long-settled locations in the temperate ecologies and latitudes of China (Millward 1998). Nevertheless, (and as exploitation, by Japanese imperialists and modern geographical surveys of that territory's soils, forests and minerals suggest) this was hardly the case for Manchuria. Yet for generations China's Manchu rulers remained at best reluctant and, at worst, negligent in placing restrictions on the mass settlement of landless Han Chinese into their well-endowed homeland or in neighbouring Mongolia (Elvin 2004).

For reasons that have not been clarified the Qing state also tried to prevent its subjects from emigrating overseas and gave them no protection whatsoever when they travelled or migrated outside the frontiers of the empire (Isett 2007). Instead the regime encouraged and even subsidized internal migration, reclamation and resettlement into regions with under and unused but cultivable land that was often poorly located with respect to waterways for irrigation, drainage and transportation. *Prima facie* this default resort to a policy of unrestrained internal migration and settlement looks like a sensible and humane but cheap way of dealing with the growing problem of otherwise poor and landless labour (Deng 2012). Yet the outcome (pushed further in an inefficient direction by rising prices for timber and wood fuel) encouraged logging and the replacement of trees and shrubs and vegetation growing on the lower slopes of hills and mountains with tea and new world and cash crops including potatoes, maize and tobacco (Marks 1998; Elvin 2004, 2012).

The empire's margin of arable land was thereby extended by the reclamation of uplands from trees and by virtually unregulated private investment in terraces, polders and dikes to capture and retain downward flows of water. Unfortunately extending the margins for cultivation at the expense of forests and onto light sandy and stony soils embodied negative externalities for the majority of the empire's workforce engaged directly, or indirectly, with arable agriculture. They became more vulnerable to uncontrollable floods in seasons of heavy and/or drought in years of light rainfall (Dixin and Chengming 2000).

Over the course of the seventeenth century the yields from crops grown by Chinese, along with farmers elsewhere in the world, also became subjected to the negative effects from the world's mini ice age (Parker 2013). This occurred at a time when unfiltered and less efficiently controlled flows of water containing stones and silt clogged channels for irrigation and drainage and lowered the levels and obstructed the passage of rivers and waterways utilized for internal trade and specialization. Traditional and omnipresent tensions between villagers, farmers, settlers and migrants sharing access to water as a common resource intensified demands and pressures for government intermediation, coordination and, above all, for higher levels of public expenditures upon the repair, maintenance and net capital formation required for the empire's irrigation, drainage and transport systems in order to cope with the pressures placed upon them by extending margins of cultivation to maintain food security for a rising population (Buoye 2000).

After an extraordinarily long and successful history as a premodern organic economy and society which coped and adapted to the takeover of the state by an alien regime, an accelerated rate of diminishing returns set in. Nevertheless, the Qing dynasty maintained the traditional laissez faire ideology and physiocratic strategy for agrarian-based development that had served the empire well for centuries, but which became increasingly untenable for an era of accelerated population growth (Spence and Mills 1979). Historical perspective reveals that the empire's prior and long economic success emanated from fortunate and diverse natural endowments, together with an extensive imperial market that had been only moderately encumbered by China's political system, framework of property rights or culture from obtaining benefits from a process akin to an agrarian form of Smithian growth (Rawski and Li 1998). This sanguine view of China's economic history implies that a critique of the political economy pursued by the Qing regime based upon comparisons (however reciprocal and cogently specified) should be tempered by a recognition that divergence with the West may well be regarded as an anachronistic comparison to contemplate. As Pomeranz recently recognized even for the most advanced region of China (Jiangnan) possibilities for the invention and/or the diffusion of western technologies for convergence towards European modes and rates of urban industrialization was a distant prospect (Pomeranz 2006, 2011).

Furthermore, it was not until late in the eighteenth century that the beginnings of control of marital fertility emerged in France. Thus, the only realistic strategies for further agrarian development that the Qing regime might conceivably have pursued (after it had consolidated its takeover of the empire in 1683) or more realistically after military campaigns in the eighteenth century had secured China's internal frontiers against nomads, would have required nothing less than fundamental reforms to the state's fiscal, financial and monetary systems to achieve (Kuroda 2013).

Such reforms would have involved a redesigned land tax based upon cadastral surveys and an enlarged bureaucracy for assessment and collection, supplemented by extensions to the range of taxes to include industry and services. These policies were hardly considered until after an avoidable Taiping rebellion nearly toppled the state between 1850–65. With sufficient revenues at its disposal, successive Qing governments could conceivably have sustained and commanded an army, of the scale and effectiveness necessary to maintain internal order across a vast expanse of territory and among heterogeneous social groups who lived as subjects of an empire under alien rule (Deng 2012).

Furthermore, a greater degree of access to enhanced flows of revenue (which was frequently discussed among the mandarins of Qing China) could have enabled that state to recruit and educate personnel, to create institutions and to mobilize resources for an altogether more effective response to the crying need to repair, maintain and extend the empire's system of natural and constructed waterways. Foundations for gains from ecologically-based specialization and trade had for centuries depended heavily upon access to and control of water for irrigation, drainage and the transportation of foodstuffs and organic raw materials. The management of water conditioned the development of inter- and intra-regional comparative advantages within which China's extensive free trade area had operated historically. Ergo informed critiques of the role of the imperial state in that vital macro-economic task cannot be dismissed as Eurocentred or inconceivable (Tvedt 2010).

Although it may be the case (as recent publications in environmental history have suggested) that by the time the Qing regime had consolidated its sovereignty over the empire and extended its frontiers it was

60    P. K. O'BRIEN

confronting not merely accelerated population growth, but an intensification of pressures from malign natural forces against a depreciating stock of capital for the access to and control of water (Perdue 1982; Will 1985). The long-established institutions for the coordination and management of China's complex system of interconnected rivers, tributaries, channels, ditches, dikes and polders was, moreover, a long way from anything that could be depicted (pace Wittfogel) as "Oriental despotism".

On the contrary and while ultimate sovereignty over the infrastructure for irrigation, drainage and waterways utilized for internal trade in food and raw materials are harnessed as a source of energy was subject to state regulation, and commands from far away Beijing, the day-to-day operations of conduits for the movement and distribution of water, as well as the repair, maintenance and extensions to these conduits was, in effect, devolved onto local authorities (villages and irrigation communities) dominated by gentry (Zelin et al. 2004; Deng 2012). Local and agrarian historians have exposed the inefficiencies of a system riddled with predictable problems of coordinating and managing a common resource, that included moral hazards and free riding as well as multiple kinds of corruption and above all, principal–agent problems in a context where the agents were scattered numerous, self-interested and locally powerful (Leonard and Watt 1992; Park 1997). While the principals (representing the state and charged to regulate a network of facilities for the control and distribution of water across an increasingly extensive and populous landscape of farmland) were few and far between (Schram 1985). Their traditional role had long been to act as inspectors and monitors of government regulations, to remain as advisers to local authorities and the gentry and operate as mediators in conflicts concerned with the distribution of water and maintenance of shared conduits for its flows onto and off private farms. As the key link in an official chain of command carrying increasing burdens of responsibility for the agrarian infrastructure of an expanded empire with insufficient revenues at their disposal and charged with the need to accord priority to the settlement of increasing numbers of landless families, their power and incentives to restrain environmental degradation could only have been limited and declining (Elvin 2004, 2010).

Unfortunately, historians will never accumulate the statistical evidence needed to measure long-term trends in public and private investment in the infrastructure of waterways and roads for agricultural production and trade in late imperial China. There is an interesting suggestion from

Pierre Etienne Will that the empire's potential for large scale spectacular projects for the control of water had been exhausted and the problem had matured into one of conservation and maintenance and piecemeal extensions to a long-established system (Will 1985). At that point in history and for an empire where political, social and economic systems confronted nature on a daily basis, the Qing regime seems to have neglected to meet its responsibilities to reform the constitutional and institutional frameworks required to maintain and, if possible, raise the output of food and organic raw materials to levels that might conceivably have placed China on a more promising trajectory towards modern economic growth by exploiting the empire's potential for even higher levels of agrarian productivity and intra-imperial trade, based upon net capital formation and better managed flows of water for irrigation and transportation.

Although the California School deserves full credit for consigning a tradition of European condescension towards the history of the Chinese empire to the basements of libraries, the Qing state and to some prior but less serious degree the late Ming regime, ultimately failed to: maintain and modernize sufficient military and naval power to provide their subjects with either sustained external security, internal order or the social overhead capital required to sustain long-established patterns of agrarian development, facilitated by Smithian growth. For millennia that pattern had depended upon extensions to China's frontier of fecund land connected to and coordinated with the management of flows of water for the irrigation of crops as well as riverine transportation required for commerce in foodstuffs, fibres, fuel, timber and manufactures that allowed the population to reap gains from trade and ecologically based specialization, both within and to an entirely limited degree, beyond the frontiers of the empire (Elvin 2010).

China's long-held position as the world's largest and most advanced organic economy began to crumble in the face of demographic pressure that emerged in the seventeenth century (Li 2007). According to Deng's adjustments to official estimates, the empire's population had risen to reach around 100 million people by the twelfth century, declined sharply to around 60% of that level during the Mongol conquest and rule and remained roughly constant for some three centuries. Thereafter it began to move upwards again at a dramatic rate to reach a level of over 400 million by 1850 (Deng 2004). Although differences in revised estimates for population remain of concern for all historians of imperial China, a consensus exists that a pronounced and persistent discontinuity occurred in its natural rate of increase, which coincided with the consolidation of political stability for the empire by an alien Qing dynasty in the late seventeenth century.

Internal peace along with economic recovery not only allowed for renewed cultivation of land abandoned during the turmoil of the Manchu takeover but enabled the new regime to pursue a strategy of military expansion along and well beyond the northern and western frontiers of the Ming empire (Perdue 2005). The Qing strategy for defence and expansion secured China against future attacks and predation by warrior tribes of nomads from the steppes of central Asia, and more than doubled its territory and increased the empire's area of potentially cultivable farmland. The new regime coped with a rapidly increasing population whose standards of living must prima facie has fallen under pressure from a serious decline in the ratio of cultivable land per capita. The options of an advanced organic economy to maintain, let alone raise, the rate of growth above the level required for food security, became far more constrained than those afflicting most populations of Western Europe at that time. They included the resettlement of landless families in Manchuria, Mongolia, Sichuan, Hunan, Anhui and other underpopulated territories incorporated, but only gradually integrated into the economy of the Qing empire (Patterson 2006). Although the regime displayed some reluctance to open up the underexploited land, forests and minerals of its homeland and adjacent Mongolia to unrestricted migration, it did encourage and, to some meagre degree, subsidize internal migration within the empire while positively discouraging emigration overseas (Isett 2007).

The regional concentration of the population changed before 1850, but the scale of internal migration to the underdeveloped and sparsely populated areas of the empire did not, however, operate as an effective safety value for the surplus families of China's densely populated regions. Incentives to move to the empire's newly acquired and underdeveloped provinces were, it seems, not strong enough nor supplemented by state expenditures on the infra-structural capital required to compensate for extending the cultivated area onto less fecund soils located in regions without easy access to supplies of controllable water for irrigation, transportation and trade (Crossley et al. 2006; Millward 1998).

Most Chinese opted to remain within the established heartlands of the empire, employed on family farms where they realized, whatever potential they possessed to increase output from the land, labour and water that they commanded by intensifying labour inputs in order to: increase the number and diversity of crops grown per annum; add more fertilizer to their soils; to allocate extra labour time to spin yarn and weave cloth from cotton fibres, ramie and silk and to engage in local, interregional and foreign trade. With entirely limited help from infrastructural investment funded, executed and coordinated by the state for some two centuries after 1650, China's peasantry managed to sustain an extraordinary increase in the size of the empire's population. That achievement seems to have occurred, moreover, without sufficient extensions to the empire's cultivated land, mass internal migration or technological shifts in a production possibility of boundaries that had, according to Mark Elvin's classical text of 1973, confined Chinese farmers to a "high level equilibrium trap" long before the Manchu dynasty consolidated its rule over the empire (Elvin 1973; Feuerwerker 1992; Deng 1999, 2012).

## References

*American Historical Review Forum.* (2002). Political economy and ecology on the eve of industrialization: Europe, China and the global conjuncture, *107*(2).

Andrade, T. (2016). *The gunpowder age: China's military innovation and the rise of the west in world history.* Princeton: Princeton University Press.

Brandt, L., & Rawski, T. (Eds.). (2008). *China's great transformation.* Cambridge: Cambridge University Press.

Brook, T. (2005). *The Chinese state in Ming society.* London: Routledge Curzon.

Brook, T. (2010). *The troubled empire: China in the Yuan and Ming dynasties.* Cambridge, MA: Harvard University Press.

Buoye, T. (2000). *Manslaughter, markets and moral economy: Violent disputes over property rights in eighteenth century China.* Cambridge: Cambridge University Press.

Chang, C. L. (1955). *The Chinese gentry: Their rule in 19th century Chinese society.* Seattle: University of Washington Press.

Chao, G. (1977). *The development of cotton textile production in China.* Cambridge, MA: Harvard University Press.

Chao, K. (1986). *Man and land in Chinese history.* Stanford: Stanford University Press.

Crossley, P. K., Siu, H. F., & Sutton, D. S. (Eds.). (2006). *Empire at the margins: Culture, frontier and ethnicity in early-modern China.* Berkeley: University of California Press.

Deng, K. (1999). *The pre-modern Chinese economy. Structural equilibrium and capitalist sterility.* London: Routledge.

64   P. K. O'BRIEN

Deng, K. (2004). Unveiling China's true population statistics for the premodern era with official census data. *Population Review, 43*, 2.

Deng, K. (2012). *China's political economy in modern times: Changes and economic consequences 1800–2000*. Abingdon: Routledge.

Deng, K., & O'Brien, P. (2015). Nutritional standards of living in England and the Yangtze Delta area circa 1644–circa 1840. *Journal of World History, 26*(2), 233–267.

Dixin, X., & Chengming, W. (Eds.). (2000). *Chinese capitalism 1522–1840*. London: Palgrave Macmillan.

Duchesne, R. (2011). *The uniqueness of western civilization*. Leiden: Brill.

Dunstan, H. (1996). *Conflicting counsels to confuse the age: A documentary history of political economy in Qing China 1644–1840*. Ann Arbor: University of Michigan Press.

Elliott, M. (2001). *The Manchu way: The eight banners and ethnic identify in late imperial China*. Stanford: Yale University Press.

Elvin, M. (1973). *The pattern of the Chinese past*. Stanford: Stanford University Press.

Elvin, M. (2004). *The retreat of the elephants: An environmental history of China*. New Haven: Yale University Press.

Elvin, M. (2010). The environmental impasse in late imperial China. In B. Womack (Ed.), *China's rise in historical perspective*. Lanham: Springer.

Elvin, M. (2012). *The pattern of the Chinese past*. Stanford: Stanford University.

Feuerwerker, A. (1973). Questions about China's early modern history that I wish I could answer. *Journal of Asian Studies, 5*. Cambridge: Cambridge University Press.

Feuerwerker, A. (1992). *State and society in eighteenth century China*. Ann Arbor: University of Michigan Press.

Feuerwerker, A. (1995). *Studies in the economic history of late imperial China*. Ann Arbor: University of Michigan Press.

Goody, J. (2010). *The Eurasian miracle*. Cambridge: Cambridge University Press.

Gray, J. (2002). *Rebellions and revolutions: China from the 1800s to 2000*. Oxford: Oxford University Press.

He, W. (2013). *Paths towards the modern fiscal state*. Cambridge, Mass: Harvard University Press.

Hirzel, T., & Kim, N. (Eds.). (2008). *Metals, monies and markets in early modern societies: East Asian and global perspectives*. Berlin: LIT Verlag Münster.

Horesh, N. (2012). *Chinese money in global context: Historical junctures between 600 BCE and 2012*. Stanford: Yale University Press.

Horesh, N. (2014). *Chinese money in global context. Historic junctures between 600 BCE and 2012*. Stanford: Stanford University Press.

Isett, C. (2007). *State, peasant and merchant in Qing Manchuria 1644–1862*. Stanford: Yale University Press.

Karaman, K., & Pamuk, S. (2010). Ottoman finances in European perspective. *Journal of Economic History, 70*, 593–629.

Kaske, E. (2017). *Crisis and austerity in Qing government finances in late eighteenth and early nineteenth century China?* Unpublished paper, University of Leipzig.

Kent, G. (2010). *The Qing governors and their provinces: The evolution of territorial government in China*. London: University of Washington Press.

Kuroda, A. (2013). What was the Silver Tael System? A mistake of China as a Silver 'Standard Country'. In G. Depeyrot (Ed.), *Three conferences on International monetary history*. Wetteren: Moneta.

Leonard, J. (1968). *Controlling from afar the Daoguang Emperors' management of the grand canal crisis 1824*. Ann Arbor: University of Michigan Press.

Leonard, J., & Watt, J. (Eds.). (1992). *To achieve security and wealth: The Qing Imperial State and the economy 1644–1911*. Ithaca: Cornell University Press.

Li, L. (2007). *Fighting famine in North China: State, market and environmental decline*. Stanford: Stanford University Press.

Liu, G. L. (2005). *Wrestling for power: The state and the economy in later imperial China, 1000–1700*. Cambridge, MA: Harvard University Press.

Ma, D. (2014). State capacity and the great divergence. *Eurasian Geography and Economics, 54*, 5–6.

Marks, R. (1998). *Tiger, rice, silk and silt: Environment and economy in Late Imperial South China*. Cambridge: Cambridge University Press.

Marks, R. (2012). *China: Its environment and its history*. New York: Rowman & Littlefield.

Millward, J. (1998). *Beyond the pass: Economy, ethnicity and empire in Qing Central Asia, 1759–1864*. Stanford: Yale University Press.

O'Brien, P. (2014). The formation of states and transitions to modern economies: England, Europe and Asia compared. In L. Neal & J. Williamson (Eds.), *The rise of capitalism from ancient origins to 1848*. Cambridge: Cambridge University Press.

Park, N. (1997). Corruption in eighteenth century China. *Journal of Asian Studies, 56*, 967–1005.

Parker, G. (2013). *Global crisis. War, climate change and catastrophe in the seventeenth century*. New Haven: Yale University Press.

Patterson, G. (2006). *Asian borderlands: The transformation of Qing China's Yunnan frontier*. Cambridge, MA: Harvard University Press.

Perdue, P. (1982). Water control in the Dongting lake region during the Ming and Qing periods. *Journal of Asian Studies, 41*, 747–765.

Perdue, P. (2005). *China marches west: The Qing conquest of central Eurasia*. Cambridge, MA: Harvard University Press.

66   P. K. O'BRIEN

Perkins, D. (1969). *Agricultural development in China 1868–1968*. Edinburgh: Aldine Publishing Company.

Peterson, W. (Ed.). (2002). *The Cambridge history of China. Vol. 9 The Ch'ing Dynasty to 1800*. Cambridge: Cambridge University Press.

Peyefitte, A. (1992). *The immobile empire*. New York: Knopf.

Pines, Y. (2012). *The everlasting empire: The political cult of ancient China and its imperial legacy*. Oxford: Oxford University Press.

Pomeranz, K. (2000). *The great divergence: China, Europe and the making of the modern world economy*. Princeton: Princeton University Press.

Pomeranz, K. (2006). Without Coal? Colonies? Calculus, counterfactuals and industrialization in Europe and China. In R. Lebow et al. (Eds.), *Unmaking the West: What if scenarios that rewrite world history*. Ann Arbor: Michigan University Press.

Pomeranz, K. (2011). *Historically speaking*. Baltimore: John Hopkins University.

Rawski, T., & Li, L. (Eds.). (1998). *Chinese history in economic perspective*. Oxford: Oxford University Press.

Rosenthal, J-L. & Wong, R. B. (2011). *Before and beyond divergence: The politics of economic change in China and Europe*. London: Harvard University Press.

Rowe, W. (2009). *China's last empire. The great Qing*. London: Belknap Press of Harvard University Press.

Schram, S. (Ed.). (1985). *The scope of state power in China*. Hong Kong: Columbia University Press.

Smith, P., & von Glahn, R. (Eds.). (2003). *The Song-Yuan-Ming transition in Chinese history*. Cambridge, MA: Harvard University Press.

Spence, J., & Mills, J. (Eds.). (1979). *From Ming to Qing*. New Haven: Yale University Press.

Struve, L. (Ed.). (2004). *The Qing formation in world historical time*. London: Harvard University Press.

Tanimoto, M., & Wong, R. B. (Eds.). (2019). *Public goods provision in the early modern economy: Comparative perspectives from Japan, China and Europe*. Oakland: University of California Press.

Tvedt, T. (2010). Why England not China and India? Water systems and the history of the industrial revolution. *Journal of Global History, 5*, 29–50.

Vries, P. (2013). *Escaping poverty. The origins of modern economic growth*. Vienna: Vienna University Press.

Vries, P. (2015). *State economy and the great divergence: Great Britain and China 1680s–1850s*. London: Bloomsbury.

Waley-Cohen, J. (1999). *The sextants of Beijing: Global currents in Chinese history*. New York: W.W. Norton.

Waley-Cohen, J. (2006). *The culture of war in China: Empire and the military under the Qing dynasty*. London: Bloomsbury.

Wang, Y. (1973). *Land taxation in imperial China, 1750–1911.* Cambridge, MA: Harvard University Press.

Will, P-E. (1985) State intervention in the administration of a hydraulic infrastructure: the example of Hubei Province in late imperial times. In S. Schram (Ed.), *The scope of state power in China.* Hong Kong: Hong Kong university press.

Wong, R. B. (1997). *China transformed: Historical change and the limits of European experience.* Ithaca: Cornell University Press.

Yun-Casalilla, B., & O'Brien, P. (Eds.). (2012). *The rise of fiscal states: A global history 1500–1914.* Cambridge: Cambridge University Press.

Zelin, M. (1984). *The magistrates' tael: Rationalizing fiscal reform in eighteenth century Ch'ing China.* Berkeley: University of California Press.

Zelin, M., et al. (2004). *Contract and property in early modern China.* Stanford: Stanford University Press.

Zurndorfer, H. (2016). China and science on the eve of the great divergence 1600–1800. *History of Technology, 29.*

CHAPTER 5

# SinoCentred Reciprocal Comparisons of Europe's and China's: Economic Growth 1650–1850

**Abstract** Perhaps the period and chronology most realistically represented as marked by divergence between Western Europe and Imperial China can be most plausibly located as the centuries between 1644 and 1846—when structural change, urbanization, technological progress and state formation became the outstanding and commonplace features of transitions to modern economic growth in several regions and countries of Western Europe. In scale and scope nothing comparable became visible in Ming and significant for Qing China where the problem confronting the imperial state was how to maintain standards of living for a rapidly increasing population. For reasons that are elaborated in this chapter, the cluster of Sinocentred analyses and narratives concerned to explain why European economies responded more effectively and efficiently to the challenges of demographic change will be elaborated, referenced and exposed as partial and inadequate as European economic history.

**Keywords** Population growth · Multilateral and Atlantic trade · Slavery · Exploitation · Bullion · Coal and energy regimes · Agricultural progress · Cotton textiles · Urban agglomeration and networks · Warfare and mercantilist competition

© The Author(s), under exclusive license to Springer Nature Switzerland AG 2020
P. K. O'Brien, *The Economies of Imperial China and Western Europe*, Palgrave Studies in Economic History, https://doi.org/10.1007/978-3-030-54614-4_5

69

After a protracted, stimulating and heuristic debate one significant conclusion has emerged from two decades of published discourse on the Great Divergence. With or without the convergence and overtaking of China by western economies, the political, geopolitical and economic policies and institutions that had carried a vast empire to a position of the world's most advanced organic economy that polity had not, however, reached a plateau of possibilities for structural change. Furthermore, and confronted by an accelerated growth in population, the empire's dynastic rulers and the wealthy gentry they protected remained incapable of providing the Chinese masses with external security, internal order and employment required for a standard of living that may not have been more than marginally above the level required for food security.

In what has now evolved to become a virtual literature of controversial analytical narratives on the Great Divergence, the California School and their followers have, moreover, tended to minimize and divert attention away from the endogenous economic problems that had emerged by late Ming times and confronted Chinese agriculture with an increasingly serious shortage of fecund land and controllable water. Their writings concentrate attention on the achievements of commerce and rural industry under the Ming and the geopolitical successes of Manchu armies in securing and extending the territorial frontiers of the empire menaced for centuries by nomads. Both these profound changes occurred, but at a time when the total number of Chinese people may have multiplied by factors variously estimated to be between 4 and 8 and reached a total that may have been in excess of 450 million people by 1850. In cycles that varied from country to country and time to time the populations of most Western European societies also experienced demographic pressures over the seventeenth and eighteenth centuries, but at natural rates of increase that most estimates suggest could have been a lot lower than the wide range of contentious figures currently in print for China (Lee and Wang 1999; Deng 2004).

Pomeranz and the California School have certainly not failed to recognize that the scale and scope of the challenge that an already advanced organic economy confronted in coping with the problems of controlling water could only have been more complex and costly to manage than those confronting the rain-fed agricultures of Western Europe. They are, moreover, also clearly aware that the prospects and potential for intra-continental seaborne trade between the urbanizing and industrializing regions and economies of western Europe and the primary producers of grains, fish, timber, mineral ores, pitch, tar, flax, hemp, wines and olives located in ecologically distinct regions of that continent were by no means exhausted or anything but marginally replaced by imports from the Americas until later in the nineteenth century. They have made a valid point that the capacities of Western Europeans to import organic raw materials, timber and minerals from the Baltic and Russia, was in part derived through multilateral trade, whereby bullion expropriated from South America was shipped to China and India, exchanged for tea, silk, porcelain and other commodities, which were then (along with American silver and Caribbean sugar) traded for the primary products of eastern Europe (Frank 1998; Hobson 2004). Nevertheless, it must also be observed that this uplift in gains from multilateral trade and specialization is not simply given by geographical endowments and locations, but are also attributable to investments in shipping and the coordination and finance of inter-continental trade by European commercial and mercantile enterprise (Gerschenkron 1966; Cipolla 1976; Crouzet 2001).

Furthermore, and what remains as a degraded hypothesis is the view (initiated and elaborated by the World Systems School of Historical Sociology) that the societies of Western Europe circumvented the kind of Malthusian problems afflicting China, India and other parts of the world economy, by importing "significant" shares of their increasing demands for food, fuel, fibres, minerals and timber from other continents on terms of trade that could be plausibly depicted as exploitative (Blaut 1993; Van Zanden 2009).

Transcontinental trade happens to be the most intensively studied branch of European economic history. It has left historians with a virtual library of publications analysing commercial connexions between Europe, Africa, Asia and the Americas, as well as an extensive array of statistics for taxed volumes and values for a range of commodities transported by sea and land into European ports. They were sold at prices that certainly rewarded merchants engaged in transcontinental commerce, with relatively high rates of return on the investments they made and services they performed to coordinate, fund and ship "luxurious commodities" (including tropical groceries, porcelain, silks and cottons from China) across continents. In retrospect, "radical" historians are prepared to represent the differential between the prices paid for these imports from Asia, Africa and the Americas and the prices received for them in Europe as extortionate. Some commodities including spices, bullion and cotton cloth and fibres, tobacco and sugar were certainly purchased on markets

72    P. K. O'BRIEN

where Europeans (aided and abetted by local middlemen) deployed coercion and monopoly powers to depress local prices below levels based on voluntary forms of exchange. Only an unknown proportion of European trade with Africa, Asia and the Americas could, however, be unambiguously and uncontentiously represented as "Western exploitation" in that derogatory sense. For most intercontinental trade the rewards could be more appropriately depicted as unequally distributed but acceptable to the Chinese, Indians, Africans, Arabs and others facilitating voluntary exchanges with Europeans. Historians have not, moreover, measured the share of the gains from trade between the Orient and Occident that accrued to Chinese or Indian middlemen.

Coercion, colonialism and imperialism colour the discussion over economic divergence in relation to the material gains and potential for growth derived by Europe's economies from the transportation of millions of Africans for forced and cheap labour on plantations in the Americas (Northrup 2010). They (as well as the enslaved native American labour who mined bullion) produced sugar, tobacco, indigo, cochineal, cotton fibres and other raw materials exported to Europe. Thus, American products relieved pressure on local agricultures in the West from growing demands for foodstuffs, organic raw materials and timber, supplied a relatively new, and land and labour-saving fibre for the diversification of the textile industry and attracted settlers who extended markets for international services and commodities manufactured in Europe (Abernethy 2000).

Few European historians have doubted that the rise and the integration of an Atlantic economy, the inclusion of America's bullion and rich natural endowments into an Atlantic economy, producing exportable surpluses of sugar, tobacco, cotton fibres and indigo with enslaved African labour, would accelerate the development of Europe's maritime economies and alleviate Malthusian pressures as and when they emerged. But they may also observe that the Qing empire, through conquest, had not only acquired much greater external security, but significantly augmented its natural resources of cultivable land, possessed very considerable and known resources of fossil fuel as well as an elastic supply of underemployed and underutilized cheap labour (Perdue 2005).

Furthermore, statistical evidence that access to imports of primary produce from the Americas provided significant relief to the growing populations of Western Europe from the kind of Malthusian pressures afflicting China has not, and most certainly cannot, be marshalled as cogently specified evidence, either from surviving bodies of trade data or from the national literatures in European demographic and agrarian history covering the period before the massive influx of American grain and other primary produce came on stream after 1873 (Etemad 2007).

Some versions of the place and status of the Americas in narratives concerned with the rise of the West and its converse—the retardation of China (and India) continue, however, to represent their discovery as a fortuitous event stimulated by a drive to augment the volumes and profits from seaborne trade with the more advanced economies of the East Indies. That view tends to be based on the well-known contingencies surrounding voyages of discovery and to neglect their foundations in a far longer and complex history of European maritime expansion overseas and the evolution of the knowledge, technologies and capital that transformed an aspiration into a possibility (Abernethy 2000; Headrick 2000, 2009; Mitterauer 2007). Yet it took prolonged investment, migration, settlement and costly imperial conflict as well as the infamous purchase and transportation of millions of enslaved Africans to labour in a new continent, to establish and consolidate its potential for colonization, settlement and commerce (Daly 2015). To evolve into an integrated and dynamic component of an Atlantic economy with sufficient potential as a source of land-saving imports and a market for exports that placed some favourably located European economies on trajectories promoting transitions to industrial market economies took centuries, not decades, to achieve (Goodman and Honeyman 1988; Mielants 2007). The historical process involved far more than the small volumes of imported calories embodied in sugar, the taxable but harmful properties of tobacco, expensive timber and animal furs underlined by the California School (Ringmar 2007). Apart from bullion and cotton fibres and dyestuffs it is not clear when and to what degree economic connexions between European economies and the Americas became significant for their transitions to modern economic growth (Bayly 2004). As late as 1830 the share of commodities imported from North and South America amounted to 30% of imports from all other continents, while the proportion of total exports had risen from 12% in 1750 to 20% by that date (Gills and Thompson 2006). Bullion certainly operated to facilitate multilateral trade and the development of financial intermediation across Europe (Flynn et al. 2003). Inputs of imported high-quality cotton fibres and indigo purchased at prices depressed by the employment of slave labour were clearly of some importance for the mechanization and accelerated the rise of cotton textile production, first in Lancashire followed by other regions in Europe. But that particular connexion was neither necessary nor sufficient for the precocious and exemplary technological transformation of that famous industry. On the contrary, the chronology and mode of its development is also consistent with the view that an indigenous belief in the "power" of machinery, promoted mechanization which inturn promoted the massive increase in European demand for cotton fibres, that was met by the rapid spread of slave plantations onto underexploited land in the tropical regions of the Americas and linked to the extension of export markets for cotton textiles (Riello 2013; Bruland et al. 2020).

There were certainly positive as well as negative forward linkages from other American imports to European industries, such as the manufacture of copper vats for boiling sugar cane. But the transplantation of potatoes, maize and other new world plants supported the maintenance of peasant farms, which at one and the same time encouraged dangerously high rates of population growth, but discouraged migration to the Americas. Conceivably the discovery of a lost continent and the gradual exploitation of its natural resources by Europeans may not have been anything other than more positive for Europe than Qing conquests and colonization of resources in central Asia ever became for the development of the Chinese empire? (Adshead 1995). Adam Smith's view that "the discovery of America and that of a passage to the East Indies are two of the greatest and most important events recorded in the history of mankind" has, as he recognized at the time, turned out to be historically correct but premature. There was little, moreover, that was merely fortuitous about the discovery of the Americas (Boorstin 1983). Eurocentrism no longer includes the assertion that the Chinese lacked the maritime knowledge and ships to sail there, but also notes the empires' production of cotton textiles depended to a high degree on imported cotton fibres from India (Chao 1977). Thus macro-economic gains from the creation, consolidation and gradual integration of an Atlantic economy cannot be plausibly represented either as fortuitous or as a major contrast with China. Distinctions between factors initiating and forces sustaining Europe's transitions to modern industrial economies must be maintained as foundational for debates about the Great Divergence (Prak and Van Zanden 2013).

Unfortunately, reciprocal comparisons between the performances of early modern Chinese and European agricultures may be impossible to conduct in ways that could lead to plausible conclusions about relative capacities to support their rising populations with structural change. Nevertheless, it can be maintained with some confidence that none of the standard up-to-date surveys of European economic and/or agrarian histories suggests that, in general, the continent's agricultural sectors failed to cope with the demographic pressures that emerged after 1650 (Broadberry and O'Rourke 2010). On the contrary, they support perceptions that the development of agriculture in several countries including England, Ireland, the Netherlands, France, Spain and Saxony displayed improvements in yields as well as the productivity of labour emanating from the diffusion of a backlog of well-established techniques such as a fallowing, improved drainage, applications of lime and marl and the introduction of new world crops (maize and potatoes) (Béaur et al. 2013). In contrast to Qing China, European farmers enjoyed an access to a larger backlog of known techniques to exploit. They were not caught in a high equilibrium trap (Jones 1987). They apparently responded to the more or less rapid growth of urban and overseas demands and rising prices of food, fodder, fuel and raw materials by extending margins for cultivation and raising yields per hectare (Bateman 2012). Contrary assertions that Europe's agricultural sectors were also running into comparably malign Malthusian crises and trajectories as China during the seventeenth and eighteenth centuries are not supported by its agrarian and demographic historians (Malamina 2009). Until well into the nineteenth century and despite the transfers of American food crops both Western Europe and the Chinese empire continued to rely upon geographically confined bases of natural resources and potential rather than transnational and intracontinental trade to meet demands from populations expanding on trend at very different rates of increase, neither of which needs to be represented as Malthusian? (*European Review of Economic History Symposium* 2008).

Thus, a larger part or emphasis in explanations for convergence linked to a Great Divergence must be attributable to Europe's latent potential for catch-up realized by the emergence of incentives for improvements to tenurial institutions as well as the diffusion of best practice techniques for the cultivation of arable land and the breeding and feeding of farm animals (Campbell and Overton 2010). Several European agricultures appear to have responded elastically to the widening of markets and to favourable shifts in the terms of trade for food, fuel and fibres which accompanied upswings in population growth, together with the

76   P. K. O'BRIEN

concentrations of people in towns (Barbier 2011). Urbanization appeared earlier and more extensively and rapidly in the Netherlands, England, North-western France and other parts of Europe than anywhere in China, including the relatively urbanized Yangtze Delta (Li and Van Zanden 2012). Eurocentred economic historians continue to regard that as an indication that specialization, the division of labour, skill formation, fiscal possibilities and prospects for technological innovation and other benefits from "urban agglomeration" became potentially more promising in Europe than China (Floud et al. 1981–2014; Roy and Riello 2019).

Turning to coal, both continents seem to have been equally well informed about its properties as a source of heat (thermal energy) for industrial and domestic purposes. British society may have been better informed about the locations and accessibility of its underground coal deposits. There is, however, no hard evidence for contrasts in the technologies used either for the mining or the potential for the transportation of coal (Wright 1984). Chinese property rights for the exploitation of sub-soil minerals may have been more complex and less secure (Scott 2008). Furthermore, neither the Ming nor the Qing state displayed any enthusiasm for the early exploitation of China's truly massive reserves of coal. They were, if anything, hostile to the spread of mining communities as potential threats to internal order (Thompson 2003).

Meanwhile, over the centuries of convergence, Europeans (particularly the British) began to explore and exploit the enormous potentialities for economic growth embodied in coal. First, and of primary importance for this debate, fossil fuel represented an increasingly elastic and significant substitute for wood—traditionally the universal material for: construction, supplies of thermal energy and domestic heat. As such the subterranean forests of both the Occident and the Orient could be exploited in order to convert land that would otherwise be cultivated to produce timber into pasture to sustain farm animals and/or arable land for the cultivation of food and fibres for human consumption (Warde et al. 2013).

Calculations by the Cambridge School suggest that by 1800 without access to coal, a truly enormous volume of wood and an extensive area of woodland would have been required to sustain existing levels of demand from British producers to generate the flows of thermal energy that had evolved by that time, to sustain a diverse range of heat-intensive manufacturing processes, and to meet demands from households for the warmth that they consumed in order to live and operate at eighteenth century standards of health and efficiency for work in towns (Wrigley 2016).

Thus the California School have received strong and convincing support from recently published interpretations of Britain's precocious transition to a modern industrial economy in terms of elastic supplies of energy (Wrigley 1988, 2016). They replicate points made by Nef as long ago as 1932. He noted how the fortuitous, fortunate and early exploitation of England's accessible and transportable endowment of coal evolved into a prominent comparative advantage that conserved labour and capital as well as land for the production of foodstuffs and raw materials. Coal thereby supported the release of labour into jobs outside agriculture and facilitated the agglomeration of an increasing proportion of the workforce in towns and cities (Nef 1964).

Nef's insights into the potential significance of coal have also, moreover, been rehabilitated and reconfigured by a new paradigm for quantification based on the kind of statistics "floated" by Braudel's estimates for volumes of energy consumed by economies as they became more urban and industrial (Braudel 1981–84). No doubt the California School may well be gratified to read that coal and other natural endowments are once again being elevated in narratives—particularly for British, but by extension—for European industrialization (Wrigley 2016). Presumably proponents of this revived interpretation will not be impressed by predictable responses from economists who remain inclined to denigrate, if not, ignore the role of natural endowments, in models constructed to explain Great as well as Little divergences over the long run.

Historians do, however, appreciate that British and subsequent European transitions to industrial market economies that led to divergences cannot be reduced to any fortuitous and superior access to local deposits of coal. At the same time they also remain aware of Europe's shift to the production and consumption of coal which became the alternative fuel for a mechanical, cheaper and more reliable form of thermal, and eventually kinetic, energy than any of the world's other sources of energy derived from human, animal, wind, timber and water power. Thus, and through a well-understood sequence of historical stages in Europe, coal became the dominant fuel for the manufacture of iron to replace reliance on timber and for the creation of steam power which provided the energy required for the mechanization of an ever-widening and more effective range of processes involved in the production and transportation of commodities and services. The presence of potentially massive deposits of fossil fuels buried underground and underwater must have incentivized the search for ways of pumping and draining water in order to mine this cheaper fuel. During a familiar sequence of technological development and improvements from Newcomen to Watt (linked to western scientific investigations into the properties of a vacuum) coal then promoted a process that transformed a mechanized water pump that facilitated the mining of minerals and fossil fuels into an "engine" that supplied the power required to operate an ever-widening range of machinery (Church 1994; Goldstone 2008).

The macro-economic spinoffs from saving land, capital, labour and animal power that accrued to economies that invested in this networked set of technologies for the supply of energy cumulated through time to become highly significant (Kellenbenz 1976). For example, it was no accident that Britain (a country with an abundant and transportable supply of this fuel and an acute shortage of timber) became the locus for the discovery, improvement and early diffusion of mechanized processes for production associated with thermal and then kinetic energy derived from coal. Although the circularity of that connexion to mechanization must be kept in view. Did access to cheap coal intensify the search for machines/engines, furnaces, chimneys, stoves, etc., to deal with opportunities that emerged in mining and utilizing coal as the most efficient source of fuel for the generation of energy and domestic heat? Alternatively, did demands for heat determine the rising price for wood which stimulated a higher elasticity of substitution of coal as the most efficient form of domestic, thermal and eventually kinetic energy create exceptionally favourable conditions for the mechanization of production and transportation? (Perrson 2010). Either way access to abundant deposits of coal for firms and households might as Pomeranz asserts, be represented as an entirely fortunate "lucky" (his depiction) and significant natural advantage for Europe? (Harris 1992; Wrigley 2016).

Nevertheless, Pomeranz will not deny that the Chinese had been well informed about the properties of coal since the Song era and (as we now realize) possessed a super abundance of coal reserves. The California School have endeavoured to formulate reasons why such rich sources of energy (that evolved historically to become a core component of England's and Europe's transition into technologically progressive industrial economies) remained underexploited in China for decades when the environmental costs of denuding the empire's hills and landscape of trees became increasingly serious (Pomeranz 2006). Several of the answers offered include such small and probably insignificant points that the Chinese obtained more of the fuel they consumed for thermal purposes from crop residues and animal dung for energy. They might have added that the population of China lived between warmer latitudes than Europeans and thus required lower levels of calorific nourishment to sustain their bodily energies for work.

Nevertheless, the core of the thesis that compared to England's (and by extension, other countries on the mainland with rich accessible and transportable endowments of coal), China could be represented as being at a serious disadvantage is beginning to look more improbable. After all the Chinese had been mining coal since the Song dynasty and continued to do so on some scale in a range of locations during the Ming and Qing times (Wright 1984). Furthermore, the literature in industrial history that systematically and reciprocally compares developments in the mining and transportation of coal in Europe with China over the centuries of Qing rule—1644–1911—lend very little if any support to views that evoke serious contrasts for delays in the exploitation of a fossil fuel for a source of energy that was: available in greater abundance, comparable in quality, accessible to the labour-intensive mining technologies of the day and perhaps as transportable by water as the coal mined in the coalfields of England, Belgium, Germany and other European locations (Thompson 2003; Xue 2007).

Throughout centuries of divergent trajectories, the imperial economy and its population depleted China's indigenous endowment of forests and woods by continuing to rely on trees and woodlands for timber for construction, and fuel for thermal energy and domestic heat which steadily reduced the natural capacity of trees to absorb and to regulate the flows of water for the production of food and raw materials (Elvin 2004). Over the same centuries, led by England, the economies of Western Europe embarked upon a strategy for the provision of thermal and kinetic energy that could "conceivably" have been pursued by Ming and Qing China. Whether or not the substitution of fossil fuels could also have incentivised a search for a mechanical solution to pump and drain water from Chinese mines was not improbable (Lebow et al. 2006). In any case, Chinese coal was being mined at shallower depths and combustibility which may have been less of a handicap than water for the exploitation of major deposits. And somehow the Qing state managed to organize the transportation of copper mined in Yunnan all the way to Beijing. The case that the empire was handicapped by relatively serious environmental disadvantages in moving to exploit the manifold and substantial advantages from shifting to an energy regime more heavily based on fossil fuels is not proven, but looks even less secure than the more widely and intensively debated reasons why an advanced and commercialized economy continued for decades to display such reluctance to mechanize industry, urbanize its workforce, and reform the policies pursued by the state to repair and extend the empire's depreciated infrastructure for the continuation of agrarian and Smithian growth in order to reach a plateau of feasible possibilities for the mechanization of industry and transportation. After all no claims have been made that the kauf system for the production of cotton textiles by Chinese households displayed signs that it was likely to mechanize its modes of production (Chao 1977; Riello 2013). Neither incentives nor scientific cultures for innovation were, it seems, pervasive in Ming or Qing China.

About a decade after Pomeranz published his seminal book on the Great Divergence, two distinguished scholars from the California School have, moreover, attempted to undermine critics, who had noticed that large differences can be observed in urbanization rates between early modern Europe and China, which required closer and more comparative analysis (Xu 2016). Otherwise this accepted and plausibly measured contrast could be read as symptoms of a long-term failure by Chinese agriculture to supply surplus food and raw materials to release labour and capital and to act as a market for commodities and services produced in towns (Rosenthal and Wong 2011).

In touch with relevant economic theory and Fernand Braudel's writings on "Europe's City Centred Economies", they have constructed an analytical narrative (unsupported by much statistical evidence) which purports to explain how, when and why the concentration of higher proportions of European populations in towns cumulated over the centuries to create contexts and conditions for higher rates of long-run economic growth (Braudel 1981–84). Surveying the historical literature on the history of European urbanization and textbook economics on network externalities, they embrace a familiar theory that urbanization operated as a major force behind the creation of favourable locations and contexts for structural change and higher standards of living in pre-modern Europe (Bairoch 1988).

Economic theory and urban history have explored the ways in which towns facilitated the expansion of demand for diverse ranges of output and consumption, promoted more refined levels of occupational specialization accompanied by higher wages for skilled and semi-skilled labour; attracted younger more motivated and educated and productive migrants from the countryside. Towns also maintained mortality from urban diseases at levels that helped to depress natural rates of increase of populations to lower and more manageable levels, and above all, provided optimal locations for the generation of scientific and technical knowledge. Furthermore, and from urban maritime locations, Europe's ports became more specialized and actively engaged with seaborne trade and transportation. This extended bases for taxation initially to support oligarchical city and regional forms of governance that evolved over time into fiscal bases for more centralized and effective states (O'Brien et al. 2001; Prak and Van Zanden 2013).

Granted that economic gains (including the all-important mechanization of European industries) can be connected to the tendency of European societies to locate a rising share of their economic activities and workforces in towns and maritime cities, that salient contrast might indeed be represented as a (or perhaps even the) key chapter for a comparative history of how convergence led to a Great and Persistent Divergence (Goldstone 2008). Comparative histories (which also take as given comparable agrarian capacities to support urbanization) could then be focussed on several inter-related questions of when, how and why Western Europe secured and retained this significant advantage over the Chinese empire (Clark 2013).

Moving on to complement the emphases that Pomeranz had accorded to coal, colonies and unequal trade, Rosenthal and Bin Wong supplement his contested explanation for divergence with reference to geopolitical features of European political economy that in their perception, embodied another significant and ultimately fortunate economic outcome that was not foreseen or intended (Rosenthal and Wong 2011; Tanimoto and Wong 2019). They find that this key contrast originated with the collapse of the Roman Empire and subsequent development over the centuries of a geopolitically fragmented system of competitive western states, afflicted by more violent social disorders and prone to persistent and protracted outbreaks of more or less destructive interludes of inter-state warfare. To cope with such universal problems of internal order and external security, Europeans erected and settled in fortified towns that protected citizens with property, human capital and liquid assets against predation. Although they had clearly not done so to a sufficient degree to deter the huge destruction of human and physical capital in the Thirty Years War and again by protracted interludes of warfare between 1792 and 1815 (Parker 2013).

Wealthy urban oligarchies then formulated rules and established institutions for the operation of economic affairs and complied with demands for taxes, credits and loans from local, regional and national authorities charged with their protection and help with the enforcement of rules for the conduct of economic affairs (Yun-Casalilla and O'Brien 2012).

In brief and over centuries, marked by inter-state mercantilist competition and warfare, Europeans constructed towns, established institutions and formed centralized states to mitigate the problems associated with economic order and afflictions from endemic and unavoidable warfare in ways and on a scale that can be contrasted with China ('t Hart 2014). For longer stretches of the empire's history, including most of the period between the accession of the Ming dynasty (1368) and the Opium War (1839–41), an imperial system of agrarian and village economies operated under more peaceful conditions. Rules and institutions were maintained for production and commercial exchange and enforced by dynastic rulers and their meritocratic bureaucracies reigning, but not ruling over, a vast territorial empire (Brook 1998, 2010). With peace, China's rulers came under limited pressures to increase revenues or borrow funds for purposes of defence or imperial aggression (Liu 2005). They felt no compulsion to interfere in the economic affairs of their subjects, except to mediate in disputes over property rights to land and oversee the maintenance of functional waterways for trade and the irrigation of crops (Zelin et al. 2004). Compared to cross-border and overseas trade in Europe, China's intra-imperial commerce was untrammelled by state regulations and conducted by merchants under a functional mix of informal and formal arrangements of their own making and often between kin located in distant parts of the celestial empire (Wong 1997; Dixin and Chengming 2000; Peterson 2002).

By European standards state expenditures and taxation (per capita, per square kilometre of territory and per mile of frontier) on the army and navy, on relief from famines, floods, droughts and poverty, on legal mediation and enforcement and, above all, on the infrastructure for production, transportation and commerce in foodstuffs and organic raw materials seems to have been meagre under both Ming and Qing regimes (Zelin 1984; Kaske 2017). Unlike Europe, the Chinese Imperial state could preside or reign over an organic economy that for centuries continued to be well endowed with a diverse and rich range of ecological resources, an infrastructure for the maintenance of rivers and canals, supported by a deferential population growing at natural rates of increase held in check by periodic disasters and infanticide (Engelen and Wolf 2005). The state also derived and actively maintained strong support from a pervasive ideology (Confucianism) which inculcated a respect for hierarchy, orderly behaviour and kin-based institutions and associations (Brook 2005). In contrast to Christianity, Confucianism never evolved into an institutionalized belief system that intervened in economic affairs as well as moral behaviour. Christianity certainly did and it also actively condoned wars over religion (Bodde 1991; Brooke 1991; Yao 2002).

Rosenthal, Wong and other sinologists have long been critical of Eurocentred writings on China's "despotic" state because they have failed to recognize the economically efficient and socially benign policies it pursued to maintain internal order, peace and a neutral stance in a political economy (a proto-Smithian strategy) for organic economies to pursue. Indeed and in the writings of the California School, the Ming and Qing regimes and their vast empires have been represented as exemplars for that kind, pattern and trajectory for "Smithian" economic progress and a benign evolution from warfare to welfare states (Wong 1997; Rawski 2001; Deng 2012).

In the course of an enlightening debate on the Great Divergence, these arguments can now be read as Sinocentred as the Eurocentred views they have so heuristically challenged. Warfare certainly became increasingly costly and detrimental for the economic development of most European polities. Nevertheless, for centuries before 1815 armed interstate conflict in the West remained as endemic and as unavoidable as smallpox. Counterfactual arguments based upon strategies for reduced levels of expenditures, taxation and borrowing by states for defence and aggression represent nothing more than the anachronistic speculations of liberal historians from another era. The problem for early modern European states in process of formation, was how to survive and if possible prosper within the confines of a mercantilist international economic order that, after 1500, expanded its reach, grasp and warlike policies to include commerce and colonization with Africa, Asia and the Americas. For European historians there is simply no viable counterfactual to contemplate. Western geopolitics were both different and economically unfortunate (O'Brien 2014; Vries 2015).

Nevertheless, in addition to the obvious benefits from victories and survival, the spinoffs and externalities obtained from the mobilization of fiscal, financial and real resources for <u>unavoidable</u> interstate warfare also embodied a range of positive linkages for the development of several economies. For example, warfare helped to form more patriotic and deferential workforces; consolidated the need for Europe's aristocratic "contractor states" to depend upon partnerships with merchants and manufacturers supplying foodstuffs, transportation, weapons and other industrial goods, for their armies and navies. Warfare raised levels of compliance with the demands of centralized states for taxes, credits, long-term loans and acceptable supplies and forms of money. It fostered a cooperative interest among ruling aristocratic and wealthy mercantile elites in the accumulation of knowledge that could become reliable enough to attract patronage for the development of sciences, technologies and skills deployed initially for armies and navies, but which also embodied prospects and potential for adaptation for more peaceful purposes. Above all, the knowledge and experience gained by way of naval and military warfare became an enduring comparative advantage for Europeans in their geopolitical conflicts with the armed forces of powers from other continents, including China. Gains from imperialism were inextricably linked to Europe's competitive mercantilism and warfare (O'Brien 2014).

To sum up: although the costs of armed conflict were high, they were unavoidable. Thus, in retrospect, European warfare may well be represented in Rosenthal and Wong's terms as an integral component of Europe's shared mercantilist and capitalist trajectory for a sequence of early transitions to industrial market economies that, in outcome, left the altogether more laudable, peaceable and theoretically efficient liberal trajectory pursued for the maintenance of stability, internal order and prosperity of the world's largest imperial economy in a condition of relative backwardness and geopolitical vulnerability (Wang 2011). Before the British Navy achieved command of the oceans and a liberal international economic order became viable, mercantilists never tired of analysing and extolling the gains of national economies could make from interstate competition that unavoidably included interludes of costly and barbaric armed conflict (Enciso 2017). Clearly there are gains of scope and scale to be gained from integrating local, regional and national economies within the political and geopolitical frontiers of larger territorial polities (Wood, 2002). Indeed that occurred for the German and Italian economies as an outcome of a reaction to French imperialism during Europe's Napoleonic war, 1803–15. Nevertheless Rosenthal and Wong might pause to consider how many of the world's other empires in situ and in operation between 1500 and 1800 have yet to succeed in providing high standards of living for their subjects?

Finally, to analyse and emphasize how protracted and costly violence attended Western Europe's earlier transitions to modern industrial economies without considering the array of variables that its historians have persuasively linked to mercantilist competition and geopolitical warfare between European states is to ignore the rules for engagement in reciprocal comparisons with China (Torres-Sanchez 2007). The analytical narrative by Rosenthal and Wong which claims to have moved the debate on to "Beyond and Before the Great Divergence" and to contrast the Qing regime with European states in allocating resources to public goods rather than protection and aggression is not convincing. It accords undue and statistically untested weight to a parsimonious but underspecified model of the range of variables and connexions (apart from warfare) that conditioned the relative propensities of European populations to migrate, to settle, engage and interact in economic activities in walled towns. Although Europeans almost certainly derived comparative advantages over China from the agglomeration of its populations in towns which plausibly promoted the formation of capital, skills and institutions for earlier transitions to modern economic growth (Braudel 1981–84; O'Brien et al. 2001). But does this perception not lead into a plausible argument that the Chinese (and other oriental empires) became and remained too extensive to be other than lightly governed by states that were possibly too infrequently challenged by the pressures of mercantilist warfare? (Wang 2011; Dincecco and Wang 2011; Dincecco and Onorato 2018). Are we not left with the meta-questions of how to frame and test hypotheses between state formation, warfare and economic growth?

## REFERENCES

Abernethy, D. (2000). *The dynamics of global dominance: European overseas empires 1415–1980*. New Haven: Yale University Press.

Adshead, S. (1995). *China in world history*. London: Palgrave Macmillan.

Bairoch, P. (1988). *Cities and economic development from the dawn of history to the present*. Chicago: University of Chicago Press.

Barbier, E. (2011). *Scarcity and frontiers: How economies have developed through natural resource exploitation*. Cambridge: Cambridge University Press.

Bateman, V. (2012). *Markets and growth in early modern Europe*. London: Routledge.

Bayly, C. (2004). *The birth of the modern world 1780–1914*. Oxford: Oxford University Press.

Béaur, G., Schofield, P. R., Chevet, J.-M., & Pérez Picazo, M. T. (Eds.). (2013). *Property rights, land markets and economic growth in the European countryside*. Turnhout: Brepols Publishing.

Blaut, J. (1993). *The colonizer's model of the world*. New York: The Guilford Press.

Bodde, D. (1991). *Chinese thought, society and science*. Honolulu: University of Hawaii Press.

Boorstin, D. (1983). *The discoverers: A history of Man's search to know the world and himself*. London: Knopf Doubleday Publishing Group.

Braudel, F. (1981–84). *Civilization and capitalism, 3 Vols*. London: Harper & Rowe.

Bruland, K., Gerritsen, A., Hudson, P., & Riello, G. (Eds.). (2020). *Reinventing the economic history of industrialization*. Montreal: McGill Queen's University Press.

Broadberry, S., & O'Rourke, K. (Eds.). (2010). *The Cambridge economic history of Europe, Vols 1 & 2*. Cambridge: Cambridge University Press.

Brook, T. (1998). *The confusions of pleasure. Commerce and culture in Ming China*. Berkeley: University of California Press.

Brook, T. (2005). *The Chinese state in Ming society*. London: Routledge.

Brook, T. (2010). *The troubled empire: China in the Yuan and Ming dynasties*. Cambridge, MA: Harvard University Press.

Brooke, J. (1991). *Science and religion: Some historical perspectives*. Cambridge: Cambridge University Press.

Campbell, B., & Overton, M. (2010). *Agricultural revolution in England: The transformation of the agricultural economy*. Cambridge: Cambridge University Press.

Church, R. (1994). The coal and iron industries, Vol. 10. In R. Church & A. Wrigley (Eds.), *The industrial revolution*. Oxford: Blackwell.

Chao, G. (1977). *The development of cotton textile production in China*. Cambridge: Harvard University Press.

Cipolla, C. (1976). *Before the industrial revolution: European society and economy, 1000–1700*. London: Routledge.

Crouzet, F. (2001). *A history of the European economy 1000–2000*. Charlottesville: University of Virginia Press.

Clark, P. (2013). *The Oxford handbook of cities in world history*. Oxford: Oxford University Press.

Daly, J. (2015). *Historians debate the rise of the west*. Abingdon: Routledge.

Deng, K. (2004). Unveiling China's true population statistics for the pre-modern era. *Population Review., 43*, 2.

Deng, K. (2012). *China's political economy in modern times: Changes and economic consequences 1800–2000*. Abingdon: Routledge.

Dincecco, M., & Wang, Y. (2011). Violent conflict and political Development over the long run: China versus Europe. *Annual Review of Political Science, 21*, 341–358.

Dincecco, M., & Onorato, M. (2018). *From warfare to wealth: The military origins of urban prosperity in Europe*. Cambridge: Cambridge University Press.

Dixin, X., & Chengming, W. (2000). *Chinese capitalism 1522–1840*. London: Palgrave Macmillan.

Elvin, M. (2004). *The retreat of the elephants: An environmental history of China*. New Haven: Yale University Press.

Encisco, A. (2017). *War, power and the economy*. Abingdon: Routledge.

Engelen, T., & Wolf, A. (Eds.). (2005). *Marriage and the family in Eurasia: Perspectives on the Hajnal hypothesis*. Amsterdam: Aksant.

Etemad, B. (2007). *La possession du monde. Poids et mesures de la colonization*. Lausanne: Editions Complex.

*European Review of Economic History Symposium*. (2008).

Floud. R. et al. (Eds.). (1981, 1994, 2004 and 2014). *Cambridge economic histories of Britain, Vol. 1*. Cambridge: Cambridge University Press.

Flynn, D. O., Giráldez, A., & Von Glahn, R. (2003). *Global connection and monetary history 1470–1800*. Aldershot: Ashgate.

Frank, A. G. (1998). *ReOrient: Global ecnomy in the Asian age*. London, University of California Press.

Gerschenkron, A. (1966). *Economic backwardness in historical perspective*. Cambridge, MA: Harvard University Press.

Gills, B., & Thompson, W. (Eds.). (2006). *Globalization and global history*. Abingdon: Routledge.

Goldstone, J. (2008). *Why Europe? The rise of the west in world history 1500–1850*. New York: McGraw Hill.

Goodman, J., & Honeyman, K. (1988). *Gainful pursuits: The making of industrial Europe, 1699–1914*. London: Edward Arnold.

Harris, J. (1992). *Essays in industry and technology in eighteenth century England and France*. Aldershot: Routledge.

Headrick, D. (2000). *When Information Came of Age. Technologies of Knowledge in the Age of Reason and Revolution, 1700–1850*. Oxford: Oxford University Press.

Headrick, D. (2010). *Power over Peoples: Technology, Environments, and Western Imperialism, 1400*. Princeton: Princeton University Press.

88    P. K. O'BRIEN

Hobson, J. (2004). *The eastern origins of western civilization*. Cambridge: Cambridge University Press.

Jones, E. (1987). *The European miracle. Environments, economies and geopolitics in the history of Europe and Asia*. Cambridge: Cambridge University Press.

Kaske, E. (2017). *Crisis and austerity in Qing government finances in late eighteenth and early nineteenth century China?* Unpublished paper, University of Leipzig.

Kellenbenz, H. (1976). *The rise of the European economy*. London: Weidenfeld & Nicolson.

Lebow, R., Tetlock, P., & Parker, G. (Eds.). (2006). *Unmaking the west: What if scenarios that rewrote world history*. Ann Arbor: Michigan University Press.

Lee, J., & Wang, F. (1999). *One quarter of humanity: Malthusian mythology and Chinese realities*. London: Harvard University Press.

Li, B., & Van Zanden, J.-L. (2012). Before the great divergence: Comparing the Yangtze Delta and the Netherlands at the beginning of the nineteenth century. *Journal of Economic History, 72,* 4.

Liu, G. L. (2005). *Wrestling for power: The state and the economy in late imperial China, 1000–1700*. Cambridge, MA: Harvard University Press.

Malamina, P. (2009). *Pre-modern European economy: One thousand years (10th–19th centuries)*. Leiden: Brill.

Mielants, E. (2007). *The origins of capitalism and the rise of the west*. Philadelphia: Temple University Press.

Mitterauer, M. (2007). *Why Europe? The medieval origins of its special path*. Philadelphia: Temple University Press.

Nef, J. (1964). *The conquest of the natural world*. Chicago: University of Chicago Press.

Northrup, D. (Ed.). (2010). *The Atlantic slave trade*. Houghton Mifflin: Lexington.

O'Brien, P., Keene, D., Hart, M., & van der Wee, H. (Eds.). (2001). *Urban achievement in early modern Europe*. Cambridge: Cambridge University Press.

O'Brien, P. (2014). The formation of states and transitions to modern economies. England, Europe and Asia compared. In L. Neal & J. Williamson (Eds.), *The rise of capitalism from ancient origins to 1848*. Cambridge: Cambridge University Press.

Parker, G. (2013). *Global crisis. War, climate change and catastrophe in the seventeenth century*. New Haven: Yale University Press.

Perdue, P. (2005). *China marches west: The Qing conquest of Central Asia*. London: Belknap Press of Harvard University Press.

Perrson, K. (2010). *An economic history of Europe*. Cambridge: Cambridge University Press.

Peterson, W. (Ed.). (2002). *Cambridge history of China, Vol. 9 The Ch'ing dynasty to 1800*. Cambridge: Cambridge University Press.

Pomeranz, K. (2006). Without coal? Colonies? Calculus counterfactuals and industrialization in Europe and China. In R. Lebow et al. (Eds.), *Unmaking the West: What if Scenarios that Rewrite World History*. Ann Arbor: Michigan University Press.

Prak, M., & Van Zanden, J-L. (2013). *Technology skills and the pre-modern economy in the west and east*. Leiden: Brill.

Rawski, E. (2001). *The last emperors: A social history of Qing institutions*. London: University of California Press.

Riello, G. (2013). *Cotton: The fabric that made the modern world*. Cambridge: Cambridge University Press.

Ringmar, E. (2007). *Why Europe was first? Social and economic growth in Europe and East Asia, 1500–1850*. New York: Anthem Press.

Rosenthal, J.-L., & Wong, R. B. (2011). *Before and beyond divergence: The politics of economic change in China and Europe*. London: Harvard University Press.

Roy, T., & Riello, G. (Eds.). (2019). *Global economic history*. London: Bloomsbury Academic.

Scott, A. (2008). *The evolution of resource property rights*. Oxford: Oxford University Press.

't Hart, M. (2014). *The Dutch wars of independence*. Abingdon: Routledge.

Tanimoto, M., & Wong, R. B. (Eds.). (2019). *Public goods provision in the early modern economy: Comparative perspectives from Japan, China and Europe*. Oakland: University of California Press.

Thompson, E. (2003). *The Chinese coal industry: An economic history*. London: Routledge.

Torres-Sanchez, R. (Ed.). (2007). *War, state and development: Fiscal military states in the eighteen century*. Navarra: Pamplona.

Van Zanden, J.-L. (2009). *The long road to the industrial revolution*. Leiden: Brill.

Vries, P. (2015). *State economy and the great divergence: Great Britain and China 1680s–1850s*. London: Bloomsbury.

Wang, Y.-K. (2010). *Harmony and war*. Chinese Confucian culture and Chinese power politics. New York: Columbia University Press.

Wang, Q. (Ed.). (2011). The California school in China. *Special Issue of Chinese Studies in History, 45*.

Warde, P., Kander, A., & Malanima, P. (2013). *Power to the people: Energy in Europe over the last five centuries*. Princeton: Princeton University Press.

Wong, R. B. (1997). *China transformed: Historical change and the limits of European experience*. Ithaca: Cornell University Press.

Wood, E. (2002). *The origins of capitalism—A longer view*. New York: Verso.

Wright, T. (1984). *Coal mining in China*. Cambridge: Cambridge University Press.

Wrigley, A. (1988). *Continuity, chance and change*. Cambridge: Cambridge University Press.

Wrigley, A. (2016). *The path to sustained growth*. Cambridge: Cambridge University Press.

Xu, T. (2016), Chinese development thinking. In E. Reinert et al. (Eds.), *Handbook of alternative theories of economic development*. Cheltenham: Elgar.

Xue, Y. (2007). A fertilizer revolution? A critical response to Pomeranz's theory of geographical luck. *Modern China, 33*, 195–229.

Yao, X. (2002). *An introduction to Confucianism*. Cambridge: Cambridge University Press.

Yun-Casalilla, B., & O'Brien, P. (Eds.). (2012). *The rise of fiscal states: A global history 1500–1914*. Cambridge: Cambridge University Press.

Zelin, M. (1984). *The magistrates' tael: Rationalizing fiscal reform in eighteenth century Ch'ing China*. Berkeley: University of California Press.

Zelin, M., Ocko, J. K., & Gardella, R. (Eds.). (2004). *Contract and property in early modern China*. Stanford: Stanford University Press.

CHAPTER 6

# Cosmographies for the Discovery, Development and Diffusion of Useful and Reliable Knowledge in Europe and China

**Abstract** This final chapter presents a survey of a protracted, persistent and perhaps unresolvable debate concerned with the roles of cultures for innovation and technological progress over the centuries of widening economic divergence between Imperial China and Western Europe. Until recently the significance of cosmographies (beliefs about the celestial, terrestrial and biological operations of the natural world) for technological innovation has not attracted interdisciplinary support as a relevant meta question to pursue, let alone the cooperation required among several highly specialized sub-branches of comparative history. That kind of history transcends not merely countries but continents, religious traditions, educational systems, ideologies and institutional frameworks promoting or obstructing the diffusion of beliefs concerned with possibilities for the comprehension of nature. My examination of an increasingly extensive volume of literature surrounding the global history of factors promoting or obstructing the development of science in pre-industrial Europe and Imperial China led me to conclude that science and technological change in the West were promoted by local endogenous forces connected to the Reconnaissance, Renaissance and Reformation as well as Europe's Christian and classical traditions.

© The Author(s), under exclusive license to Springer Nature Switzerland AG 2020
P. K. O'Brien, *The Economies of Imperial China and Western Europe*, Palgrave Studies in Economic History, https://doi.org/10.1007/978-3-030-54614-4_6

91

# 92   P. K. O'BRIEN

**Keywords** Science · Technology · Cosmology · Natural philosophy · Reconnaissance · Renaissance · Reformation · Christianity · Confucianism · Aristotle · Copernicus · Newton · Universities · Republics of letters · Meritocracy · Needham

Towns were then places from which useful and reliable knowledge emerged (Nelson 1993). Pomeranz has recognized that the debate surrounding his seminal book had not engaged seriously enough with the importance of connexions between the development of science and technological innovation for economic divergence. That seems surprising because even before Herbert Butterfield published his classical study of *The Origins of Modern Science 1300–1800* in 1949 claims that science and technology had played highly significant roles in the economic and geopolitical rise of the west was often central to western claims for cultural superiority over the Orient (Butterfield 1949; Nakayama 1984; Duchesne 2011). Eurocentric writings suggest that progress and innovation in these related spheres of human endeavour had been a virtual monopoly of western societies since the classical era of Greece and Rome. That view has, however, been degraded by an ongoing programme of historical research into Science and Civilization in China initiated by Joseph Needham in 1954, which has published some 25 volumes locating and demonstrating the precedence of Chinese discoveries in their conjoined histories (Ronan and Needham 1981; Ropp 1994). Along with comparable programmes on the histories of science and technology for Medieval Islam and India claims that the locus for discovery, development and diffusion of knowledge that evolved and matured in ways that enhanced the potential of economies to produce ever more diverse volumes of commodities and services at lower costs of production was essentially a western contribution to world history has become untenable (Needham 1969, 1970; Arrault and Jami 2001; Nordhaus and Romer 2018).

The historical destruction of that myth has, however, left us with a view that the locus for scientific comprehension and technological innovation shifted from Asia to Western Europe by the end of the fifteenth century (Ropp 1994; Davids 2012). That shift remains as a core concern for Needham, Sivin and other eminent sinologists as well as historians concerned with the scientific and technological innovation in other oriental cultures and civilizations (Liu 1995; Sivin 1995). Their concerns seem to have been marginalized by scholars otherwise inclined to align their views with positions taken by the California School in the Divergence Debate (Frank 1988; Lieberman 2009; Marks 2012). One way or another evasion implicitly takes the fashionable post-modern position that in all its essentials, modern western science was "socially and economically constructed" (Golinski 1998). This "social constructivist" paradigm which has for decades dominated the history of science starts from the premise that materialist explanations for the rise of the west are sufficient to account for its modern emergence, development and location (Hacking 1999). That view is, moreover, reinforced by historians who continue to maintain that until late in the nineteenth-century connexions between science and technology remained tenuous enough to ignore as a significant factor behind Europe's early modern convergence to and divergence from the levels of productivity and standards of social welfare maintained for millennia by the Chinese empire (Inkster 1991; Inkster and Deng 2004; Liu 1995; Epstein and Prak 2008).

Nevertheless, it is necessary to insist that this albeit heuristic volume of scholarship has not disposed of the need to engage with analytical historical narratives that seek to explain when, how and why conceptions of the natural world held by Europe's educated, wealthy and political elites became relatively favourable to technological innovations introduced into that sub-continent's systems for production (Bedini 1999). It is necessary to enquire why similar connexions and institutions did not emerge on any significant scale before the twentieth century in other parts of a globalizing world economy? (Mokyr 2002, 2017; Cohen 2011; Davids 2012; O'Brien 2009, 2013, 2019, 2021).

Recovering from the onslaughts of post-modern nihilism, histories of science are now, however, becoming integrated with histories of religion to support hypotheses that suggest the consolidation of monotheistic Christendom in Western Europe generated beliefs and cultures among its elites that could (as Weber, Butterfield and Needham posited) be represented as promotional for the development of a functional cosmography for the comprehension of the natural world (Weber 1951; Tremlin 2006; Harrison 2010).

This occurred before the Reformation, but after Roman Catholicism had consolidated its role as Europe's hegemonic religion that operated to suppress all but one set of beliefs about the operations of nature in favour of "revealed truths" for which its hierarchy retained a monopoly of interpretation (Brooke 1991; Tremlin 2006). Nevertheless,

94 P. K. O'BRIEN

as the supranational cultural hegemon in conflict with monotheistic Islam, confronting popular fantasies about the natural world as well as religious heresies and competing for authority with secular rulers, the papacy and its bishops found it expedient to establish, patronize and control institutions for the higher education of clergy and secular elites (de Ridder-Symoens and Rüegg 1996; Gascoigne 1998). Europe's medieval universities offered curricula that included education in classical modes of conducting arguments in law, medicine and theology as well as a corpus of Greek and Roman speculations in natural philosophy concerned to construct general theories to explain the operations of the celestial, terrestrial and biological spheres of a universe that the church insisted was divinely created and ordered by a Christian God (Bullough 2004; Hannan 2009; Lowe and Yasuhara 2017).

In recent years scholars investigating the origins of modern science have rehabilitated this tradition of classical and post-classical intellectual endeavours to represent and understand the natural world. They have revealed how far and how deeply European comprehension of the motions of the sun, moon planet and stars had reached before the publication of a seminal book on astronomy by Copernicus in 1543 introduced a new paradigm for observation and mathematical speculation about the celestial sphere which contradicted and undermined the authority of the Church and its ecclesiastical institutions on (of all matters) the operations of the "heavens" (Grant 2007; Lindberg 2008; Penprase 2011; Gaukroger 2010).

Any serious challenge to the orthodox teachings of the Church embodied in its scriptures and beatified classical texts (including the Bible, the Gospels, the wisdom of the saints as well as the canonical, but expurgated writings of a small set of classical authors such as Galen, Hippocrates, Pliny, Euclid, Ptolemy and above all Aristotle was not taken lightly (Stark 2001). Ignored and/or repressed as heresy it took more than a century to spread across the range of knowledge (terrestrial, mechanical, biological as well as astronomical) that came to be held, believed and accepted by an increasing proportion of Europe's wealthy, powerful and educated men (Lindberg and Numbers 1986). Intellectual historians may not be able to estimate the proportions of western elites who gradually embraced and reconciled "proto-scientific" with religious views of the natural world and became optimistic about prospects for its manipulation. Their numbers rose at rates that varied from country to country and town to town. Historians will, however, agree that their comprehension of the natural world matured significantly between the times of Copernicus and Newton (Barnes 2000; Grant 2004; Gaukroger 2010; Cohen 2011).

Stages in the formation and influence of useful and reliable knowledge also depended upon the diffusion of printed books which formed a basis not merely for the circulation of new ideas and insights, but for conversations, correspondence, debate and meetings of associations and societies for discussions of natural philosophy and prospects for improvements to techniques and technologies utilized for primary production, manufacturing industry, trade, transportation, human health and welfare, as well as weapons for warfare (Huff 1993; Smith and Schmidt 2007; Baten and Van Zanden 2008).

With posts within and/or the wealth required to exercise patronage outside institutions for higher education Europe's urban intellectuals formed networks that have been labelled as Republics of Letters, dedicated to the analysis and understanding of the workings of God's natural world (O'Brien 2009; Mokyr 2017). They shared a common dissatisfaction with revealed truths as the way of comprehending that world and scepticism towards the canonical status of a limited range of Aristotelian and classical explanations for all natural phenomena. They questioned and widened agendas for education and systemic investigations to include: the age, size, shape, geography and limits of planet earth; movements of the sun, moon, stars, seas and tides; climates, earthquakes, minerals, chemical substances, soils, plants, animals, fish and human anatomy (Jacob 1997). They engaged in debates concerned with mathematical and rational methods for the study of law, medicine and even theology which maintained its hegemonic but uneasy relationship with natural philosophy (Lloyd 2009; Huff 2011; O'Brien 2013; Mokyr 2017).

Furthermore, their security, status and credibility as conveyors and purveyors of more useful and reliable knowledge was fortuitously advanced by three major historical episodes which extended the base of knowledge accessible to Europeans and seriously undermined the status of ecclesiastical elites and intellectuals with vested interests in upholding the sanctity of religious and scholastic interpretations of Greek texts purporting to represent both revealed truths and revered classical wisdoms about nature (Hodgson 1993).

First and of primary importance was the Reformation, not only because Protestant theology has been represented as clearly more accommodating

96    P. K. O'BRIEN

for the reconfiguration of natural philosophy but because the Reformation and the horrendous wars it provoked degraded the authority of any single or singular religious hierarchy to pronounce on investigations into the natural world for the whole of western Christendom (Cohen 1994; Rublack 2017).

Secondly, that power had already been weakened over the fifteenth century by major additions and contradictions to the range and scope of medieval knowledge about the world that followed from Iberian voyages of discovery. As Europe's merchants and mariners engaged more intensively in commerce with other continents their observations began to replace not only folk fantasies and classical texts on the geography of the universe, but uninformed opinions of their size and scale, their populations, fauna and flora, minerals, tradeable commodities and alien but potentially useful know-how (Hopkins 2002; Headrick 2009; Hart 2008).

Apart from the momentous discovery of a lost continent and the increasing flows of commodified knowledge and observations imported by sea into European ports from Africa and Asia as well as the Americas, the fall of Constantinople to Ottoman armies in 1453 led to a migration of scholars into Italian and other cities on the mainland carrying little known books by Greek authors that contained alternative philosophical speculations about the natural world to beatified Aristotelianism (Grafton 1992; Rossi 2001).

This geopolitical event augmented the range and volume of classical texts that became accessible for debate among scholars and educated elites engaged with ancient and revered humanistic and natural philosophy. It stimulated philological analyses which revealed errors in the works of Aristotle and exposed the fragility of a scholastic, canonical and circumscribed body of ancient wisdoms that were 2000 years old. They included only a selected and expurgated sample of a range of competing cosmographies written by Greek and developed by Islamic philosophers who had long ago endeavoured to understand and to think systematically about the universe (Gaukroger 2006).

In retrospect, the history of cultures inhabited by generations of early modern European elites can be represented as a progression towards a cosmography that in outcome and effect embodied distinctive advantages for the development of science that had virtually no parallels in other parts of the world (Lloyd 2009). As a product of the Roman empire, medieval Christendom's elite culture remained hostile to pagan thought about the universe, but nevertheless embraced a version of monotheism that over the centuries accorded an unusual amount of space and status for the accumulation of observations, investigations and speculations about the natural world—provided they remained congruent with the "truths" already revealed and expounded in doctrines contained in sacred and canonical texts, interpreted and approved by the ecclesiastical hierarchy of a Roman Catholic church (Bona 1995; Noble 1997; Grant 2004).

That evolution was neither linear in trend nor revolutionary in pace and diffusion. As intellectual history it was marked by conflicts between revealed truths and a corpus of publications that survived from Greco-Roman times that included translations commentaries and elaborations on those texts by Islamic philosophers (Montgomery 1998; Cohen 2011). In practice and for centuries the Church and its universities dealt with Europe's classical intellectual heritage by a combination of repression and reconciliation which became increasingly difficult to sustain in the wake of the augmented flows of commodities, observations and knowledge imported into Western Europe as benefits from voyages of discovery and from migrations of intellectuals promoted by the advance of Ottoman armies and internal migrations across countries within Europe (Grant 2004; Dear 2006). In tension between revealed truths on the one side and alternative ways of comprehending and thereby manipulating the natural world for material and secular purposes on the other, a widening strand within natural philosophy came into an altogether more serious conflict with the authority of the Church over the moral and spiritual doctrines and purposes of Christianity (Bona 1995; Feingold 2002). That Reformation led to schisms in religious beliefs and the formation of rival protestant churches and states.

In the course of more than a century of horrendous warfare over religion and national identities, balances of power between religious and secular authorities shifted in favour of centralized states in search of knowledge for power (Bullough 2004; Gillespie 2008). Diverse forms of Christian beliefs and churches competed for allegiance from Europe's monarchs, aristocracies and wealthy elites. Ecclesiastical control over the universities and the hegemony of theology over other faculties diminished. Curricula for a Christian education widened, not only to include reformed sets of religious beliefs and rituals, but embraced a variety of classical and revised texts for the study of mathematics, and natural philosophies that superseded the long-established tradition of Aristotelianism and its predictable decline into scholasticism (Gascoigne

1998). Paradoxically Europe's reformation at one and the same time: purified and intensified religious fundamentalism, while extending Christianity's discourse in theology to include natural philosophy and the nature of God's designs for his Universe (MacCulloch 2003). Overall the Reconnaissance, Renaissance and the Reformation created spaces within Catholic and Protestant Europe where educated elites could reconcile their spiritual beliefs with the institutionalized pursuit and patronage of knowledge maturing into a recognizable scientific cosmology that became potentially more hospitable for the production of useful and reliable knowledge (Field and James 1993; Dear 2006).

In scale and scope nothing analogous to Europe's trajectory for the formation of knowledge during this early modern period has(as yet) been documented for the intellectual histories of the Mughal Empire, the Romanov and Ottoman Dominions, Japan or China (Bala 2006) Thus, for no clear reason not much historical evidence has emerged after two decades of debate on a pre-industrial world of "surprising resemblances", that systematically compares the cosmographies embraced by oriental as well as occidental elites (Montgomery and Kumar 2016). Thus Needham's famous but unanswered question must, therefore, logically retain its place of high status and significance for the Divergence Debate (Needham et al. 2004). Unless that is the gradual evolution followed by a discernible acceleration in the penetration and spread of proto-scientific beliefs into the cultures of Europe's elites could be plausibly represented as some kind of "superstructure" for an economically and socially constructed "scientific revolution" that improbably appeared without intellectual antecedents (Liu 2009; Wootton 2015). Otherwise it will not be feasible to dismiss or denigrate contrasts in the evolution of scientific cosmographies as irrelevant for the analysis of divergent trends technological innovation in China and Western Europe (Cohen 1994; Hishimoto et al. 1995).

From their perspectives (as eminences grise for the history of Chinese science) neither Joseph Needham nor Nathan Sivin underrated the religious and cultural origins and significance and of Europe's scientific revolution. Sivin saw it as a new western mentality "shaped by science that led the educated to take an interest in manufacturing and led artisans (along with everyone else to begin reasoning abstractly about facts, procedures, commodities and labour to an extent unprecedented in human history" (Sivin 1995). Both scholars brought extraordinary erudition to bear on the foundation of a historiographical tradition that has essentially documented the primacy of Chinese science and technology for centuries before 1500 and opened up an unresolved discussion about its retardation compared to Western Europe for centuries thereafter (Selin 1997; Lloyd and Sivin 2002; O'Brien 2013; Mokyr 2017).

Apart from the tendency of some allies of the California School to evade or deny the relevance of this particular reciprocal comparison for the divergence debate several "Sinocentred" arguments have been published that can be read as serious scholarly endeavours to question the sense and degree to which the cosmology embraced by the Empire's ruling elites could be convincingly represented as conservative or indifferent towards the progressive and promotional aspects of science and sciences that were developing in the West during Ming and Qing times (Elman 2000, 2005).

But any critiques for the "failures" of Chinese science and technology to retain parity with the West must be prefaced and tempered by two facts. The first (elaborated and documented by Mark Elvin) is that no style or method of scientific investigation into the natural world in Western Europe during the early modern period has been recorded as absent in China (Inkster and Deng 2004). Under the category of Gewu Chinese literati studied reflected and published manuals on *The Crafting of 10,000 Things* of practical use and value in their own way and on "their own terms" (Elman 2005; Schafer 2011). The possible scope, scale and potential cosmographical significance of this recorded flow of printed words will be discussed below (Brokaw and Chow 2005). Meanwhile the relatively small scale of published books in per capita terms compared to Europe underlines but qualifies the economic significance of Elvin's point that China's traditions for systematic investigations into the natural world certainly included examples of methodologies diffusing, albeit it more extensively and with greater effect, in the West (Selin 1997; Baten and Van Zanden 2008).

Furthermore, the scope and scale of the Empire's overall investment in endeavours devoted to the formation of useful, reliable and potentially productive knowledge was constrained (perhaps to some significant degree) in two ways: first, by the incentives confronting young men with the secondary education, skills, talents and motivations required to allocate time and kin money to the pursuit of such knowledge, and secondly, by a tradition maintained dynasty after dynasty to recruit the bureaucracy employed to run an extensive territorial empire on the basis of results displayed in imperial examinations (Elman 2005).

The curriculum for this laudably meritocratic system exercised a dominant influence on the mission, form and content of secondary and higher education for the sons of Chinese elites and for a minority of talented students from lower down the social scale whose education was collectively funded by their kin. The Empire's education system was closely regulated to serve the political purposes of an imperial state that relied more on moral and ideological power than European-style coercion and religion to maintain stability and internal order (Nakayama 1984). Ideally, the credentials achieved endowed graduates recruited to serve the Empire with the prestige and authority derived from their status as a meritocracy implementing the decrees and orders of dynasties of emperors with mandates to rule, maintained by force but believed to be somehow derived from heaven (Peterson 1980; Elman 2000).

The content of the education they received in order to obtain positions and promotions in China's imperial administration and/or the status of literati was based upon a set of interrelated moral principles enshrined in ancient philosophical texts which (as Jesuit missionaries to China appreciated) could be plausibly represented as analogous to the moral codes embodied in Christendom's sacrosanct old and new testaments (Ner 1981; Yang 1990). Over the centuries, by way of selective adaptations from rival systems of belief (including Buddhism, Daoism and Monism, the ideology cum "theology" of Ming and Qing China had matured into a code for righteous behaviour framed by the writings of Confucius (Bodde 1991; Yao 2002; Bol 2008). At the highest levels of education this code evolved historically to include commentaries, critiques and classical texts of a curriculum for: higher education, a mark of social status that transcended birth and wealth and credentials for admission, status and power exercised in the service of the state (Rawski 1979; Davids 2012). Neo-Confucian texts which were analysed using philological methods by the best and brightest young minds in China instilled a quasi-spiritual reverence for ancient authorities and in theory inculcated virtues that embodied personal enlightenment through humanistic and didactic forms of study (Yung 1982; Elman and Woodside 1994).

From Eurocentred perspectives, the modes of teaching and content of the education maintained by the Empire's institutions for higher education, particularly their concerns with personal behaviour, social stability and political order all seem to be less than hospitable towards the development of a cosmography that promoted far more effective investigations into the operations of the natural world (Lloyd 1996; Lloyd and Sivin 2002). In China that kind of knowledge was neither protected for personal gain by patents of monopoly, awarded with prizes by the state or regarded as anything like as prestigious as classical commentaries and writings that were located and published and discussed within a neo-Confucian paradigm that contributed to harmonious family life, a deep respect for ancestors, stability of the social order and benign incorruptible governance for a huge territorial empire (Henderson 1984; Yang 1990).

By late Ming times some Chinese intellectuals began to question the utility and hegemony of traditional learning and with limited signs of success recommended that more elevated the status be accorded to utilitarian education (Brook 2010). Others advocated the study of knowledge embodied in commodities imported into the empire by European merchants or conveyed as books to the court officials by Jesuit missionaries as part of a tolerated but futile endeavour to convert the Chinese elites to a Roman Catholic religious and cosmographical view of the universe (Wright 1984; Kim 2010). Predictably alien proposals for imperial reform to the mode and content the education of Chinese elites failed perhaps because the Jesuit conduit for the diffusion of Europe's advanced scientific knowledge was limited, compromised and undermined by their religious bias against the new astronomy associated with Copernicus and Galileo (Elman 2005). That view remains contentious. It is by no means clear that Chinese philosophers were impressed one way or the other by foreign observations on planetary circulation (O'Brien 2013). Resistance to reform from an alien Manchu dynasty to modify, let alone overturn, neo-Confucian cosmography about an interconnected, harmonious, moral and political order embracing all things on earth including man and his organic relations with nature, seems more likely to have operated as a far greater conservative force against change, than the ambivalent reluctance of a small group of Jesuits to pass on Europe's most innovative scientific ideas to a Manchu regime with a record of vacillation and antipathy to opening China to the West (Li et al. 1982). Its legitimacy to rule could be undermined if it began to regard classical Chinese traditions as anachronistic and in anyway inferior to "barbarian" modes of thought (Deng 2012).

Nevertheless, flows of publications containing useful and reliable knowledge pertaining to both indigenous but increasingly foreign "things" of immediate practical and economic importance continued to appear and diffuse in print within a cosmography that remained virtually intact until the fall of the Empire in 1911 (Selin 2003; Meyer-Fong 2007; Zurndorfer 2009). Compared to Europe that cosmography has been represented by a distinguished historian of Chinese science as "a scattered landscape of individual reactions rather than a unified or linear narrative of knowledge in the making" (Schafer 2011).

Under the Qing Chinese intellectuals certainly continued to allocate time and resources to "evidential research" and some of that knowledge undoubtedly matured and contributed to technological improvements (McDermott 2006; Golas 2015). Nevertheless, the mindsets, vocabularies and conceptual frameworks they brought to the enormously complex task of transforming an organic economy experiencing Malthusian problems can continue to be regarded as inadequate and conservative (Qian 1985; Lloyd 1996). "Things" continued to be studied less for their contributions to the comprehension of the natural world and potentially useful knowledge and more for their qualities, authenticity and provenance within a cosmography that remained deferential towards the dominant tendency in neo-Confucianism to conceive of man as but a part of nature and nature as one harmonious whole in which all things continued to be investigated through the prisms of such concepts as li, ying and yang and to be correlated and connected (Bodde 1991; Vogel and Dux 2010). As Needham recognized, "the Chinese wise before their time had worked out an organic theory of the universe which included nature and man, Church and state and all things past, present and to come". Poignantly he added that unlike their European counterparts (including most of the names who dominate histories of seminal contributions to Europe's Scientific Revolution) the Chinese "lacked confidence that the code of Nature could be unveiled and read because there was no assurance that a divine being ever more rational from ourselves had ever formulated a code capable of being read" (Needham 1969, 1970). A venerable tradition in the history of western science (currently under revival) which treats the cultural and religious foundations of modern science with historicized respect could only agree with his insight (Harrison 2010). In any case, the current status and standing of modern Chinese science has not been traced back to the cosmographical foundations of its golden age (Xu 2016). Paradoxically by this our time of climate change and pandemics, Needham's depiction of it as "wise" begins to look percipient?

# REFERENCES

Arrault, A., & Jami, C. (Eds.). (2001). *Science and technology in East Asia: The legacy of Joseph Needham*. Liege: Brepols.

Bala, A. (2006). *The dialogue of civilizations in the birth of modern Science*. New York: Palgrave Macmillan.

Barnes, M. (2000). *Stages of thought: The co-evolution of religious thought and science*. Oxford: Oxford University Press.

Baten, J., & Van Zanden, J-L. (2008). Book production and the onset of economic growth. *Journal of Economic Growth, 13*, 217–235.

Bedini, S. (1999). *Patrons, artisans and instruments of science 1600–1750*. Aldershot: Ashgate/Variorum.

Bodde, D. (1991). *Chinese thought, society and science*. Honolulu: University Hawaii Press.

Bol, P. (2008). *Neo-confucianism in history*. Cambridge, MA: Cambridge University Press.

Bona, J. (1995). *The Word of God and the language of man: Interpreting nature in early modern science and medicine*. Maddison: Wisconsin University Press.

Brokaw, C., & Chow, K. (Eds.). (2005). *Printing and book culture in late imperial China*. Berkeley: University of California Press.

Brook, T. (2010). *The troubled empire: China in the Yuan and Ming dynasties*. Cambridge, Mass: Harvard University Press.

Brooke, J. (1991). *Science and religion: Some historical perspectives*. Cambridge: Cambridge University Press.

Bullough, V. (Ed.). (2004). *Universities, medicine and science in the medieval west*. Aldershot: Ashgate.

Butterfield, H. (1949). *The origins of modern science 1300–1800*. London: The Free Press.

Cohen, F. (1994). *The scientific revolution: A historiographical inquiry*. Chicago: Chicago University Press.

Cohen, F. (2011). *How modern science came into the world. Four civilizations. One 17th century breakthrough*. Amsterdam: University of Chicago Press.

Davids, K. (2012). *Religion, technology and the great and little divergences. China and Europe compared. c. 700–1800*. Leiden: Brill.

Dear, P. (2006). *Revolutionizing the sciences: European knowledge and its ambitions*. Basingstoke: Palgrave Macmillan.

Deng, K. (2012). *China's political economy in modern times: Changes and economic consequences 1800–2000*. Abingdon: Routledge.

Deng, K., & O'Brien, P. (2021). The Kuznetsian Paradigm and the Study of Global Economic History. Department of Economic History, London School of Economics. Working Paper 321.

De Ridder-Symoens, H., & Walter Rüegg, W. (Eds.). (1996). *A history of the university in Europe*. Cambridge: Cambridge University Press.

104   P. K. O'BRIEN

Duchesne, R. (2011). *The uniqueness of western civilization.* Leiden: Brill.
Elman, B., & Woodside, A. (Eds.). (1994). *Education and society in late imperial China 1600-1900.* Berkeley: University of California Press.
Elman, B. (2000). *A cultural history of civil examinations in late imperial China.* Berkeley: University of California Press.
Elman, B. (2005). *On their own terms: Science in China 1550–1900.* Cambridge, MA: Harvard University Press.
Epstein, S., & Prak, M. (Eds.). (2008). *Guilds, innovation and the European economy 1400–1800.* Cambridge: Cambridge University Press.
Feingold, M. (Ed.). (2002). *The new science and Jesuit science: Seventeenth century perspectives.* Dordrecht: Kluwer Academic Publishers.
Field, J., & James, A. (1993). *Renaissance and revolution: Humanists, scholars, craftsmen and natural philosophers in early modern Europe.* Cambridge: Cambridge University Press.
Frank, A. G. (1988). *ReOrient: Global economy in the Asian age.* London: University of California Press.
Gascoigne, J. (1998). *Science, politics and universities in Europe 1600–1800.* Aldershot: Ashgate.
Gaukroger, S. (2006). *The emergence of scientific culture: Science and the shaping of modernity 1210–1685.* Oxford: Oxford University Press.
Gaukroger, S. (2010). *Science and the shaping of modernity 1660–1760.* Oxford: Oxford University Press.
Gillespie, M. (2008). *The theological origins of modernity.* Chicago: Chicago University Press.
Golas, P. (2015). *Picturing technology in China from earliest times to the twentieth century.* Hong Kong: Hong Kong University Press.
Golinski, J. (1998). *Making natural knowledge: Constructivism and the history of science.* Cambridge: Cambridge University Press.
Grafton, A. (1992). *New world's ancient texts: The power of tradition and the shock of discovery.* Cambridge, Mass: Harvard University Press.
Grant, E. (2004). *Science and religion from Aristotle to Copernicus 400BC–AD 1550.* Baltimore: Johns Hopkins University Press.
Grant, E. (2007). *A history of natural philosophy from the ancient world to the nineteenth century.* Cambridge: Cambridge University Press.
Hacking, I. (1999). *The social construction of what? Cambridge.* Mass: Harvard University Press.
Hannan, J. (2009). *God's philosophers: How the medieval world laid the foundations for modern science.* London: Icon Books Ltd.
Harrison, P. (Ed.). (2010). *The Cambridge companion to science and religion.* Cambridge: Cambridge University Press.
Hart, J. (2008). *Empires and colonies.* Cambridge: Polity Press.

Headrick, D. (2009). *Power over people's, technology and environment: Western imperialism*. Princeton: Princeton University Press.

Henderson, J. (1984). *The development and decline of Chinese cosmology*. New York: Columbia University Press.

Hishimoto, K., Jami, C., & Skar, L. (Eds.). (1995). *East Asian science: Tradition and beyond*. Kyoto: Kansai University Press.

Hodgson, M. (1993). *Rethinking world history*. Cambridge: Cambridge University Press.

Hopkins, A. (Ed.). (2002). *Globalization in world history*. London: Pimlico.

Huff, T. (1993). *The rise of early modern science. Islam, China and the West*. Cambridge: Cambridge University Press.

Huff, T. (2011). *Intellectual curiosity and the scientific revolution*. Cambridge: Cambridge University Press.

Inkster, I. (1991). *Science and technology in history. An approach to industrial development*. New Brunswick: Macmillan.

Inkster, I., & Deng, K. (Eds.). (2004). *Special issue of history of technology vol. 29*. London: Continuum.

Jacob, M. (1997). *Scientific culture and the making of the industrial west*. Oxford: Oxford University Press.

Kim, Y. (2010). *Confucian scholars and specialized scientific knowledge in traditional China*. East Asian Science: Technology and Society.

Li, G., et al. (Eds.). (1982). *Explorations in the history of science in China*. Shanghai: Chinese Classics Publishing House.

Lieberman, V. (2009). *Strange parallels, Vol. 2. Mainland mirrors, Europe, Japan, China, South Asia and the islands*. Cambridge: Cambridge University Press.

Lindberg, D., & Numbers, R. (Eds.). (1986). *God and nature: Historical essays on the encounter between Christianity and science*. Berkeley: University of California Press.

Lindberg, D. (2008). *Science in the middle ages*. Chicago: Chicago University Press.

Liu, G. (2009). Cultural logics for the regime of useful knowledge during Ming and early Qing China. *History of Technology, 29*, 29–56.

Liu, J. (1995). The Needham Puzzle. Why the industrial revolution did not originate in China. *Economic Development and Cultural Change, 43*, 269–292.

Lloyd, G. (1996). *Adversaries and authorities*. Cambridge: Cambridge University Press.

Lloyd, G. (2009). *Disciplines in the making: Cross cultural perspectives on elites, learning and innovation*. Oxford: Oxford University Press.

Lloyd, G., & Sivin, N. (2002). *The way and the word: Science and medicine in early China and Greece*. New Haven: Yale University Press.

Lowe, R., & Yasuhara, Y. (2017). *The origins of higher learning and the early development of universities*. London: Routledge.

106   P. K. O'BRIEN

MacCulloch, D. (2003). *Reformation: Europe's house divided*. London: Allen Lane.

Marks, R. (2012). *China: Its environment and its history*. New York: Rowman & Littlefield.

Mote, F. (1999). *Imperial China 900–1800*. Cambridge, MA: Harvard University Press.

McDermott, J. (2006). *A social history of the Chinese Book*. Hong Kong: Hong Kong University Press.

Meyer-Fong, T. (2007). The printed world: Books, publishing, culture and society in late imperial China. *Journal of Asian Studies, 66*, 787–817.

Mokyr, J. (2002). *The gifts of Athena*. Princeton: Princeton University Press.

Mokyr, J. (2017). *A culture of growth*. Princeton: Princeton University Press.

Montgomery, S. (1998). *Science in translation: Movements of knowledge through cultures and time*. Chicago: Chicago University Press.

Montgomery, S., & Kumar, A. (2016). *A history of science in world cultures*. London: Routledge.

Nakayama, S. (1984). *Academic and scientific traditions in China, Japan and the West*. Tokyo: University of Tokyo Press.

Needham, J. (1969). *The Great titration: Science and society in East and West*. Toronto: Allen & Unwin.

Needham, J. (1970). *Clerks and craftsmen in China and the West*. Cambridge: Cambridge University Press.

Needham, J., Robinson, K. G., & Elvin, M. (Eds.). (2004). *Science and civilization in China Vol. 7 Part III General conclusions and reflexions*. Cambridge: Cambridge University Press.

Nelson, R. (Ed.). (1993). *National innovation systems*. Oxford: Oxford University Press.

Ner, de B. (1981). *Confucian orthodoxy and the learning of mind and heart*. New York: Columbia University Press.

Noble, D. F. (1997). *The religion of technology: The divinity of man and the spirit of invention*. New York: Alfred A. Knopf.

Nordhaus, W. & Romer, P. (2018). Integrating nature and knowledge into economics (*Royal Swedish Academy of Sciences Nobel Prize Lecture*).

O'Brien, P. (2009). The Needham question updated: A historiographical survey. *History of Technology, 29*, 7–28.

O'Brien, P. (2013). Historical foundations for a global perspective on the emergence of a western European regime for the discovery of development and diffusion of useful and reliable knowledge. *Journal of Global History, 8*, 1–24.

O'Brien, P. (2019). *Cosmographies for the discovery, development and diffusion of useful and reliable knowledge in pre-industrial Europe and late Imperial China. A survey and speculation*. VSWG 128/2021–22, 289.

Penprase, B. (2011). *The power of the stars: How celestial observations have shaped civilizations*. London: Springer.

Peterson, W. (1980). Chinese science, philosophy and some attitudes towards knowledge about the realm of heaven. *Past and Present, 87*.

Qian, W.-Y. (1985). *The great inertia: Scientific stagnation in traditional China*. London: Croom Helm.

Rawski, E. (1979). *Education and public literacy in China*. Ann Arbor: Michigan University Press.

Ronan, C., & Needham, J. (1981). *The shorter science and civilization in China*. Cambridge: Cambridge University Press.

Ropp, P. (Ed.). (1994). *The heritage of China*. Berkeley: University of California Press.

Rossi, P. (2001). *The birth of modern science*. Oxford: Oxford University Press.

Rublack, U. (2017). *The Oxford handbook of protestant reformations*. Oxford: Oxford University Press.

Selin, H. (Ed.). (1997). *Encyclopaedia of the history of science, technology and medicine in non-western cultures*. Dordrecht: Springer.

Selin, H. (Ed.). (2003). *Nature across cultures: Views of nature and the environment in non-western cultures*. Dordrecht: Springer.

Schafer, D. (2011). *The crafting of 10,000 things. Knowledge and technology in seventeenth-century China*. Chicago: Chicago University Press.

Sivin, N. (1995). *Science in ancient China: Researches and reflections*. London: Variorum.

Smith, P., & Schmidt, B. (2007). *Making knowledge in early modern Europe: Practices, objects and texts 1400–1800*. Chicago: Chicago University Press.

Stark, R. (2001). *One true God: Historical consequences of Monotheism*. Princeton: Princeton University Press.

Tremlin, T. (2006). *Minds and Gods: The cognitive foundations of religion*. Oxford: Oxford University Press.

Vogel, H., & Dux, G. (2010). *Concepts of nature: A Chinese-European cross-cultural perspective*. Leiden Brill.

Weber, M. (1951). *The religion of China*. Glencoe: Free Press.

Wootton, D. (2015). *The invention of science*. London: Harper.

Wright, T. (1984). *Coal mining in China*. Cambridge: Cambridge University Press.

Xu, T. (2016). Chinese development thinking. In E. Reinert et al. (Eds.), *Handbook of alternative theories of economic development*. Cheltenham: Elgar.

Yang, D. (1990). China's traditional mode of thought and science. *Studies in Chinese Philosophy, 22*.

Yao, Xinzhong. (2002). *An introduction to Confucianism*. Cambridge: Cambridge University Press.

Yung, K. (1982). Natural knowledge in a traditional culture: Problems in the structure of Chinese science. *Minerva, 20*.

Zurndorfer, H. (2009). China and science on the eve of the great divergence 1600–1800. *History of Technology, 29,* 81–101.

CHAPTER 7

# Debatable Conclusions

**Abstract** Some twenty years of stimulating controversy on the Great Divergence conducted in large part within the Kuznetsian paradigm for modern economic history remains heuristic to read and contemplate because it exposes the limitations of that paradigm for reciprocal comparisons across continents for premodern times. The debate returns historians, economists and other social scientists to the unwelcome realization that transitions to modern economic growth are path-dependent and have occurred among the nations of the world in sequences heavily conditioned by their geographical endowments and their complex and diverse histories of political, geopolitical and institutional development. Comparisons and controversy remain heuristic ways of understanding long run growth and locating contemporary controversies in their historiographical contexts helps us to appreciate their significance.

**Keyword** Eurocentrism · Long-run growth · Chronology · Climacteric · Malthus · Smith · Elvin · Pomeranz

After two decades of scholarly intellectual discourse among historians and social scientists with credentials and claims to the expertise required to engage in what has developed into the most famous modern example of

© The Author(s), under exclusive license to Springer Nature
Switzerland AG 2020
P. K. O'Brien, *The Economies of Imperial China
and Western Europe*, Palgrave Studies in Economic
History, https://doi.org/10.1007/978-3-030-54614-4_7

109

the comparative approach to global history, debate on the Great Divergence is now virtually over (Vries 2016; Parthasarathi and Pomeranz 2016).

"History without controversy is not history". By stimulating debate over the Great Divergence the California School may well lay claim to several significant historiographical achievements. First and foremost and at a propitious time in the history of China and the world economy, they brought the late imperial economy (and in its wake other Asian empires—Mughal, Ottoman and Safavid) into the frame of historical investigations and analytical narratives concerned with the institutional, economic, technological, scientific, political and geopolitical factors and forces behind the rise of the west (Daly 2015).

In consolidating a historiography of China's centuries of prior primacy in all these material spheres of human endeavour, the California School have effectively degraded the last vestiges of Eurocentrism and restored imperial China to the position it long held as the world's most advanced organic economy, until the economies and polities of western Europe first converged and then diverged for centuries in ways and at a pace that left the peoples of China with inferior standards of living, geopolitical insecurity and internal instability (Daly 2015, 2019).

Unfortunately the volume and quality of macro-economic and demographic data available in records for Ming and Qing China do not allow either Euro or Sinocentred historians to locate or construct the viable statistically-based historical chronology required to analyse conjunctures of divergence and convergence between the economies of China and the West (Deng and O'Brien 2015, 2016; but vide Pomeranz 2017; and Broadberry et al. 2018).

That all-important chronology could provide the framework for an analytical narrative to account for the historical origins and subsequent widening of divergence between the economies of late imperial China and Western Europe. Alas all that we have access to are libraries of books, articles and debates, constructed by scholars with credentials in the economic histories of imperial China and/or Europe (Deng and O'Brien 2021). Apart from crucial differences in the range and quality of basic data available for reciprocal comparisons, the printed secondary sources accessible to those who cannot read classical Chinese are mainly in European languages because very few academics from Chinese universities have ventured to become engaged with a debate concerned with the status and quality of an imperial past that predates the foundation of a People's Republic in 1949 (Wang 2011; Garcia and de Sousa 2018). Thus, the debate remains unavoidably based on a sample of secondary sources produced by scholars with posts at western universities (Wang 2011; Vries 2015; Roy and Riello 2019).

Nevertheless the protracted engagement from a group of distinguished economic historians dedicated to scholarly debate has generated lessons for their colleagues and social scientists who wish to engage in comparisons across space and time with themes in global history that remain as universally significant as the wealth and poverty of nations. The divergence debate has exposed the fragility of parsimonious models manufactured by economists to explain the complexities behind two contrasting histories of inter-related environmental, geopolitical, political, demographic and cultural forces that placed the organic economies of China and western Europe on different trajectories leading to several centuries of Great and Prolonged Divergence (Macfarlane 2014; Deng and O'Brien 2015, 2016, 2021).

More than coal (which the empire possessed in abundance). Beyond conquests across frontiers for control over cultivable land and other natural resources which anyway occurred on a large scale but to an under-exploited degree. Despite a climacteric in the formation of scientific and technological knowledge; (which China could and did eventually import and adapt from the west). The rich scholarly literatures on the pre-industrial histories of Imperial China and Western Europe has led me to a conclusion that the Great Divergence can be plausibly attributed basically to two endogenous (Chinese) factors: namely, the penalties of an early start leading to the depletion of favourable natural endowment (Deng 1999; Elvin and Liu 1998; Elvin 2004). Secondly the inertia that accompanied success, together with the strength of an otherwise benign but detached imperial rule that provided limited encouragement to search for scientific and technological solutions to China's Malthusian problems (Elvin and Liu 1998; Elvin 2004; Deng and O'Brien 2021).

After two decades of an enlightening debate these factors cannot be avoided or evaded with references to a highly selective and short list of "fortuitous" factors and forces, particular and peculiar to western Europe, such as deposits of coal, the discovery and exploitation of the Americas, the collapse of Roman, Carolingian and other territorial empires on the mainland or warfare and differential expenditures on public goods (Wang 2011). After reading but a fraction of the rich and historical literature that has done so much to further the diffusion of global history this Euro-centred author (who cannot, alas, read Chinese) became convinced that the most objective way to construct an analytical narrative for the timing and protracted persistence of divergence between Imperial China and Western Europe, is to begin by recognizing the limitations of otherwise laudable endeavours to construct narratives in global economic history in the absence of primary statistical sources required to conduct the exercises in quantification required by the Kuznetsian paradigm for the study of long-run economic growth (Kuznets 1966, 1971; Allen et al. 2011). Might it not be more heuristic to recognize salient contrasts between two economies located at the extremities of Eurasia? During an era dominated by agrarian and organic forms of production, the environmental spaces, ecological conditions and natural endowments accessible to Chinese populations seem prima facie to have been more conducive to the cultivation and processing of a wider range of commodities for consumption, trade and specialization than was the case for the populations of Europe (Elvin 2004). As these natural endowments evolved into comparative advantages for local and regional specialization, Chinese communities across a vast space, communicating in a common language and sharing a common culture, saw advantages in complying with rules and ideologies maintained by dynasties of warriors who promised to provide them with the political stability, internal order and external security required for the extension and integration of markets across the world's largest contiguous territorial empire (Deng 2015). Sometime (?) before the Qing regime of Manchu warriors took over the governance of that empire, signs of environmental deterioration and depletion of natural resources became discernible and worsened when the growth of the population accelerated after the new Manchu regime consolidated its reign over greatly extended swathes of territory in central Asia (Rowe 2009; Von Glahn 2016).

In short the message from this unavoidably superficial survey of a library of secondary sources on Imperial China published in English is that the famous controversy over the Great Divergence launched by the California School may have contributed more to our understanding of the Rise of the West than they have added to the analytical narratives and more cautious approach to quantification and comparative methods contained in monographs published by previous generations of Chinese and Western scholars in their endeavours to comprehend and communicate explanations for the onset and prolonged retardation of Imperial China (Elvin 1973, 2004; Elvin and Liu 1998; Deng 1999, 2015). The penalties of an early start, the emergence of Malthusian pressures and the burdens of funding and managing such a spatially enormous empire cannot alas be measured and rigorously compared with Western Europe. Nevertheless, they continue to remain as key chapters for analytical narratives of divergence between China and the West which, as Herodotus would recognize, represents nothing more than another long cycle in global history that at this moment of climate change and pandemic is transmuting into a convergence that is, alas, beginning to look less desirable to celebrate (Grinin and Korotayev 2015).

## References

Allen, R., Bengtsson, T., & Dribe, M. (2011). Wages, prices and living standards in China in comparison with Europe, Japan and India. *Economic History Review, 64*, 8–38.

Broadberry, S., Guan, H., & Li, D. D. (2018). China, Europe and the great divergence: A study in historical national accounting. *Journal of Economic History, 78*, 955–1000.

Daly, J. (2015). *Historians debate the rise of the west*. Abingdon: Routledge.

Daly, J. (2019). *The rise of western power*. London: Bloomsbury.

Deng, G. (1999). *The premodern Chinese economy*. London: Routledge.

Deng, K. (2015). *Mapping Chinese growth and development over the long run*. Singapore: World Scientific Publishing.

Deng, K., & O'Brien, P. (2015). Nutritional standards of living in England and the Yangtze Delta area circa 1644–circa 1840. *Journal of World History, 26*(2), 233–267.

Deng, K., & O'Brien, P. (2016). Establishing statistical foundations for the great divergence: A survey and critique of relative wage levels for Ming-Qing China. *Economic History Review, 69*(4), 1057–1082.

Deng, K., & O'Brien, P. (2021). The Kuznetsian Paradigm and the Study of Global Economic History. Department of Economic History, London School of Economics. Working Paper 321.

Elvin, M. (1973). *The pattern of the Chinese past*. Stanford: Stanford University Press.

Elvin, M. (2004). *The retreat of the elephants: An environmental history of China*. New Haven: Yale University Press.

Elvin, M., & Liu, T.-J. (Eds.). (1998). *Sediments of time: Environment and society in Chinese history*. Cambridge: Cambridge University Press.

Garcia, M., & de Sousa, L. (2018). *Global history and the new polycentric approaches*. Singapore: World Scientific Publishing.

Grinin, L., & Korotayev, A. (2015). *Great divergence and great convergence.* Cham: Springer.

Kuznets, S. (1966). *Modern economic growth.* New Haven: Yale University Press.

Kuznets, S. (1971). *The economic growth of nations.* Cambridge, Mass: Harvard University Press.

Macfarlane, A. (2014). *The invention of the modern world.* Les Brouzils: Fortnightly Press.

Parthasarathi, P., & Pomeranz, K. (2016). *The great divergence debate.* Vide www.warwick.ac.uk/fac/arts/history/ghcc/event/parthasarathi-Pomeranz-text.docs.

Pomeranz, K. (2017). The Data We Have vs. the Data We Need. A comment on the Divergence Debate. The NEP-HIS Blog.

Rowe, W. (2009). *China's last empire: The great Qing.* London: The Belknap Press of Harvard University Press.

Roy, T., & Riello, G. (Eds.). (2019). *Global economic history.* London: Bloomsbury Academic.

Von Glahn, R. (2016). *The economic history of China from antiquity to the nineteenth century.* Cambridge: Cambridge University Press.

Vries, P. (2015). *State economy and the great divergence: Great Britain and China 1680s–1850s.* London: Bloomsbury.

Vries, P. (2016). *What we know and do not know about the great divergence?* at the Beginmng of 2016. Historische Mitteilungen der Ranke-Gesellschaft 28 (2016), 249 -297. University of Vienna.

Wang, Q. (Ed.). (2011). The California school in China. *Special Issue of Chinese Studies in History, 45.*

Wang, Y.-K. (2011). *Harmony and war. Chinese confucian culture and Chinese power politics.* New York: Columbia University Press.

# Correction to: The Economies of Imperial China and Western Europe

**Correction to:**
**P. K. O'Brien,** *The Economies of Imperial China and Western Europe*, **Palgrave Studies in Economic History, https://doi.org/10.1007/978-3-030-54614-4**

The initial version of this book inadvertently neglected to incorporate a list of corrections, which has now been rectified.

---

The updated version of the book can be found at https://doi.org/10.1007/978-3-030-54614-4

© The Author(s), under exclusive license to Springer Nature Switzerland AG 2021
P. K. O'Brien, *The Economies of Imperial China and Western Europe*, Palgrave Studies in Economic History, https://doi.org/10.1007/978-3-030-54614-4_8

# INDEX

**A**
Abernethy, D., 72, 73
Acemoglu, D., 12, 34, 41, 42
Adshead, S., 9, 35, 74
agrarian knowledge, 35, 39, 40, 75
agricultures, 35, 37, 40, 75, 77
Allen, R., 24, 25, 112
Americas, 21, 33, 73, 74
Andrade, T., 6, 53
Arrault, A./Jami, C., 92
Atlantic trade, 73, 74

**B**
Bairoch, P., 11, 80
Bala, A., 98
Barbier, E., 33, 35, 76
Barnes, M., 95
Barrow, J., 4
Bateman, V., 22, 75
Baten, J./Van Zanden, J-L., 95, 99
Baumol, W., 18, 19
Bayly, C., 73

Béaur, G., 75
Bedini, S., 93
Berg, M., 3, 5
Black, J., 5
Blaut, J., 71
Blue, G., 3, 5–7
Bodde, D., 83, 100, 102
Bol, P., 8, 100
Bolt, J./Van Zanden, J-L., 23
Bona, J., 97
Boorstin, D., 74
Brandt, L./Rawski, T., 26, 35, 49
Braudel, F., 11, 77, 80, 85
Bray, F., 34, 36
Brenner, R./Isett, C., 25
Breuninger, H., 6, 34
Broadberry, S., 11, 23
Broadberry, S. et al., 20, 21, 23, 110
Broadberry, S./Gupta, B., 23
Broadberry, S./O'Rourke, K., 8, 11, 20, 33, 75
Brokaw, C./Chow, K., 99
Brooke, J., 83, 93

© The Editor(s) (if applicable) and The Author(s), under exclusive
license to Springer Nature Switzerland AG 2020
P. K. O'Brien, *The Economies of Imperial China
and Western Europe*, Palgrave Studies in Economic
History, https://doi.org/10.1007/978-3-030-54614-4

# 116  INDEX

Brook, T., 35, 37, 49, 52, 82, 83, 101
Brook, T./Blue, G., 3, 5–7
Bruland, K., 74
Brunt, L., 23
Bullough, H., 94, 97
Butterfield, H., 92, 93

## C

California School, 19, 20, 25, 37, 38, 48, 49, 61, 70, 73, 77, 78, 80, 83, 93, 99, 110, 112
Campbell, B./Overton, M., 75
capital formation, 34, 53, 58, 61
Chang, C.L., 55
Chao, G., 39, 74, 80
Chao, K., 56
China and Chinoiserie, 4
  dynasties, 4, 8, 25, 63, 82, 99, 100, 112
  Imperial, 2, 4, 7, 11, 18–24, 34, 39, 60, 61, 110–112
  Peoples' Republic, 2
chronology, 19–23, 25, 74, 110
Church, R., 78
Church, R./Wrigley, A., 78
Cipolla, C., 71
Clark, P., 81
coal and energy, 21, 33, 76–79, 81
Cohen, F., 93, 95–98
Cohen, P., 10
Confucianism, 7, 9, 83, 101, 102
Cranmer-Byng, J., 6
Crossley, P., 56, 62
Crouzet, F., 71
cultures, 3, 4, 11, 21, 80, 92, 93, 96, 98

## D

Daly, J., 12, 18, 73, 110
Davids, K., 92, 93, 100

Dawson, R., 3, 4, 7
Dear, P., 97, 98
Deaton, A./Heston, A., 23
de Jong, H./Van Ark, B., 23
Deng, K., 2, 12, 26, 34, 50, 53–55, 57, 59–61, 63, 70, 83, 101, 112
Deng, K./O'Brien, P., 21–25, 110, 111
de Ridder-Symoens, H./Rüegg, W., 94
diffusion of knowledge, 92
Dincecco, M./Onorato, M., 85
Dincecco, M./Wang, Y., 85
Dixin, X./Chengming, W., 6, 32, 58, 82
Duchesne, R., 9, 11, 48, 92
Dunstan, H., 26, 50, 56

## E

East India Company, 3
Eckstein, A., 2
Elliott, M., 50
Elman, B., 36, 99–101
Elman, B./Woodside, A., 100
Elvin, M., 6, 8, 10, 25, 34, 35, 38, 40, 41, 57, 60, 61, 63, 79, 99, 111, 112
Elvin, M./Liu, Ts'ui-jung, 38, 40, 41, 111
Encisco, A., 84
Engelen, T./Wolf, A., 83
environmental depletion, 6, 35, 41, 49, 111, 112
Epstein, S./Prak, M., 93
Etemad, B., 73
Eurocentrism, 3
examinations, 99
exploitation, 71, 72
external security, 6, 7, 9, 37, 50, 61, 81

## INDEX 117

**F**
Fairbank, J., 9
Feingold, M., 97
Ferguson, N., 9, 11
Feuerwerker, A., 9, 21, 22, 25, 50, 53–55, 63
Field, J./James, A., 98
fiscal and financial institutions and administration, 50–52, 55, 56, 59, 84
Floud, R. et al., 20, 76
Flynn, D.O., 73
Francks, P., 3, 11
Frank, A.G., 3, 7, 10, 11, 71, 93

**G**
Garcia, M./De Sousa, L., 111
Gascoigne, J., 94, 97
Gates, H., 35
Gaukroger, S., 94–96
GDP, 20, 37, 51
geopolitics, 70, 84, 85
Gernet, J., 6, 34
Gerschenkron, A., 71
Gillespie, M., 97
Gills, B./Thompson, W., 73
Goldstone, J., 11, 18, 19, 23, 38, 78, 81
Golinski, J., 93
Goodman, J./Honeyman, K., 73
Goody, J., 11, 18, 34, 49
Grafton, A., 96
Grant, E., 94, 95, 97
Great Divergence, 2, 70
Gregory, J., 18
Grigg, D., 33
Grinin, L./Korotayev, A., 2, 113

**H**
Hacking, I., 93
Hannan, J., 94

Harrison, P., 93, 102
Hatcher, J./Stephenson, J., 23, 24
Hayami, A./Tsubouchi, Y., 37
Headrick, D., 73, 96
Henderson, J., 101
Hirzel, T./Kim, N., 55
Hishimoto, K., 98
Hobson, J., 8, 9, 11, 18, 33, 71
Hodgson, M., 95
Hopkins, A., 96
Horesh, N., 55, 56
Howell, M., 21
Huang, P., 35, 37, 41
Huff, T., 95

**I**
imperialism, 6, 53, 57, 72, 84, 85
index numbers, 23
India, 3, 5, 11, 24, 50, 71, 73, 74, 92
Inkster, I., 93
Inkster, I./Deng, K., 93, 99
institutions, 11, 20, 21, 49, 85
intellectuals, 4, 5, 95
internal and external migration, 57, 63
internal order, 6, 7, 36, 37, 61
irrigation system, 34, 38, 58–61
Isett, C., 25, 57, 62. *See also* Brenner, R./Isett, C.

**J**
Jacob, M., 95
Japan, 3, 11, 98
Jesuits, 4, 5, 101
Jiangnan, 39, 58
Jones, D., 3–5, 7, 8
Jones, E., 8, 10, 21, 33, 75

**K**
Kander, A., 36. *See also* Warde, P.

118  INDEX

Kander, A./Malamina, P., 76
Karaman, K./Pamuk, S., 51, 52
Kaske, E., 54, 55, 82
Kellenbenz, H., 78
Kent, G., 49, 51, 65
Kim, Y., 101. *See also* Hirzel, T./Kim, N.
Korotayev, A., 2, 113
Kuroda, A., 22, 24, 55, 59
Kuznets, S., 20, 112

**L**
Landes, D., 10, 11
Lebow, R., 19, 21, 39, 79
Lee, J./Wang F., 35, 70
Leonard, J./Watt, J., 48, 50, 60
Li, B./Van Zanden, J-L., 23, 76
Lieberman, V., 8, 18, 37, 93
Li, G., 101
Li, L., 40, 61. *See also* Rawski, T./Li, L.
Lindberg, D., 94
Lindberg, D./Numbers, R., 94
Liu, G., 98
Liu, G.L., 82
Liu, J., 92, 93
living standards, 22, 24
Lloyd, G., 95, 96, 100, 102
Lloyd, G./Sivin, N., 99, 100
Lowe, R./Yasuhara, Y., 94

**M**
Macartney, Lord, 3, 5
MacCulloch, D., 98
MacFarlane, A., 18, 19, 111
Mackerras, C., 4
Ma, D., 52. *See also* Van Zanden, J-L./Ma, D.
Maddison, A., 20, 21, 23
Malamina, P., 33, 34, 75. *See also* Kander, A.; Warde, P.

Malthusian, 33, 35, 37, 38, 40, 41, 48, 52, 71, 72, 75, 102, 111, 113
Malthus, T., 41
Maoism, 2, 7
Marks, R., 10, 33, 34, 37, 41, 57, 93
Marks, S., 11, 19
Marx, K., 6, 7
Mazumdar, S., 35
McDermott, J., 102
mercantilism, 21, 48, 49, 82
merchants, 4, 82
Meyer-Fong, T., 101
Mielants, E., 73
Millward, J., 57, 62
Mitterauer, M., 73
Mokyr, J., 93, 95, 99
Mongols, 33, 52
Montgomery, S., 97
Montgomery, S./Kumar, A., 98
Mote, F., 4
multilateral trade, 71
Mungello, D., 4, 5

**N**
Nakayama, S., 92, 100
Naquin, S./Rawski, E., 25
natural disasters, 53
natural endowments, 11, 21, 35, 58, 72, 77
natural philosophy, 94, 95
Needham, J., 9, 92, 93, 98, 102. *See also* Ronan, C./Needham, J.
Nef, J., 77
Nelson, R., 92
Ner, de B., 100
Noble, D., 97
Nordhaus, W./Romer, P., 92
Northrup, D., 72

# INDEX 119

## O

O'Brien, P., 51, 81, 83–85, 93, 95, 99, 101. *See also* Deng, K./O'Brien, P.; Yun-Casalilla, B./O'Brien, P.

Opium wars, 4

O'Rourke, K. *See* Broadberry, S./O'Rourke, K.

## P

Parker, G., 58, 82

Park, N., 50, 60

Parthasarathi, P., 3, 19

Parthasarathi, P./Pomeranz, K., 110

Patterson, G., 53, 62

Penprase, B., 94

Perdue, P., 3, 33, 41, 53, 60, 62, 72

Perez, M./De Sousa, L., 2

Perkins, D., 54

Perrson, K., 22, 78

Peterson, W., 50, 82, 100

Peyefitte, A., 48

Phillips, J., 3

Pines, Y., 55

Pomeranz, K., 2, 10, 11, 19, 22, 25, 33, 37–40, 49, 54, 58, 59, 70, 78, 80, 81, 92, 110

population growth, 6, 52, 53, 58, 60, 74, 75

Prak, M./Van Zanden, J-L., 8, 74, 81. *See also* Epstein, S./Prak, M.

## Q

Qian, W-Y., 102

Qing state, 3, 6

quantification, 20

## R

Rawski, E., 83, 100. *See also* Naquin, S./Rawski, E.

Rawski, T./Li, L., 25, 35, 39, 58. *See also* Brandt, L./Rawski, T.

Reconnaissance, 98

Reformation, 93, 95, 98

regions, 18, 20, 23, 25, 33, 35, 36, 39, 40, 57, 58, 62, 70, 71, 74

religion, 6, 83, 93, 97, 100

Renaissance, 98

retardation, 3, 18, 19

rice, 34

Riello, G., 74, 80. *See also* Roy, T./Riello, G.

Ringmar, E., 2, 19, 21, 73

Ronan, C./Needham, J., 92

Ropp, P., 92

Rosenthal, J-L./Wong, R.B., 49, 80, 81, 83–85

Rossi, P., 96

Rowe, W., 26, 41, 48, 55, 56, 112

Roy, T./Riello, G., 18, 19, 76, 111

Rublack, U., 96

## S

Sachsenmaier, D., 5

Schafer, D., 99, 102

Schram, S., 60

science and religion, 6, 93

scientific and technical knowledge, 48, 81, 92, 111

Scott, A., 36, 76

Selin, H., 99, 101

Shi, Z., 26, 36

Sierferle, R./Breuninger, H., 6, 34

silver, 71

Sivin, N., 92, 98. *See also* Lloyd, G./Sivin, N.

Smith, A., 74

Smithian growth, 80

Smith, P., 53. *See also* Smith, P./Malthus, T.; Smith, P./Schmidt, B.; Smith, P./Von Glahn, R.

120 INDEX

Smith, P./Malthus, T., 5
Smith, P./Schmidt, B., 95
Smith, P./Von Glahn, R., 53
So, B., 39–41
social constructivist science, 93
Spence, J., 4, 15
Spence, J./Mills, J., 52, 58
Stark, R., 94
State revenues and expenditure, 36,
    50–53
Staunton, G., 4
Stiglitz, J., 23
Struve, L., 53

**T**
Taiping rebellion, 55, 59
Tanimoto, M./Wong, R.B., 49, 81
technology, 76
Temple, R., 4
textiles, 39, 80
't Hart, M., 82
Thompson, E., 76, 79. *See also* Gills,
    B./Thompson, W.
Torres-Sanchez, R., 85
Toynbee, A., 7
trajectories, 25, 40
Tremlin, T., 93
Tvedt, T., 41, 59
Twitchett, D./Mote, F., 35

**U**
universities, 94, 97
urbanization, 76, 80, 81
useful knowledge, 9, 102

**V**
Van Ark, B./de Jong, H., 23
Vanhaute, E., 21
Van Zanden, J-L., 34, 71. *See also*
    Baten, J./Van Zanden, J-L.; Bolt,

J./Van Zanden, J-L.; Li, B./Van
    Zanden, J-L.; Prak, M./Van
    Zanden, J-L.; Van Zanden,
    J-L./Ma, D.
Van Zanden, J-L./Ma, D., 20, 22, 23
Vogel, H./Dux, G., 102
Von Glahn, R., 9, 11, 19, 26. *See also*
    Smith, P./Von Glahn, R.
Vries, P., 2, 3, 8, 18, 21, 22, 36, 48,
    52, 56, 83, 110, 111

**W**
wages, 23, 25
Waley-Cohen, J., 49, 55, 56
Wang, Y-C., 50
Wang, Y-K., 84, 85, 111. *See also*
    Dincecco, M./Wang, Y-K.
Warde, P., 33, 76
warfare, 81, 82
Watt, J./Leonard, J., 25, 48, 50, 60
Weber, M., 8, 93
welfare, 22, 53, 83
wells, 34
Wells, H.G., 7
Western European economies, 21, 23,
    54
Will, P-E., 36, 40, 60, 61
Wong, R.B., 10, 11, 36, 38, 49, 51,
    53, 54, 82, 83. *See also* Rosenthal,
    J-L./Wong, R.B.
Wood, E., 10, 21, 84
Wootton, D., 98
World Systems, 71
Wright, M., 3, 4
Wright, T., 76, 79
Wrigley, A., 77, 78. *See also* Church,
    R./Wrigley, A.

**X**
Xu, T., 80, 102
Xue, Y., 79

## Y

Yang, D., 100, 101
Yangtze, 23, 25, 76
Yao, X., 83, 100
Yun-Casalilla, B./O'Brien, P., 51, 82

Yung, K., 100

## Z

Zelin, M., 50, 55, 60, 82
Zurndorfer, H., 49, 101

Printed by Printforce, United Kingdom